INDIANS
OF
NORTH AMERICA

INDIANS
OF
NORTH AMERICA

The Eight Culture Areas
and How Their Inhabitants Lived
Before the Coming of the Whites

Paula Angle Franklin

Foreword by Professor Morton H. Fried
Columbia University

Line drawings by Ken Woodard

David McKay Company, Inc.
New York

Library of Congress Cataloging in Publication Data

Franklin, Paula Angle, 1928-
Indians of North America.

Includes index.
SUMMARY: An overview of eight areas where the North
American Indian lived, describing daily life, clothes,
homes, hunting, and culture.
1. Indians of North America—Juvenile literature.
[1. Indians of North America]   I. Woodard, Ken.
II. Title.
E77.4.F7   970'.004'97   78-4379
ISBN 0-679-20700-7

7 8 9 10
Manufactured in the United States of America

CONTENTS

FOREWORD

By Morton H. Fried
Department of Anthropology
Columbia University

It was very early that October morning, almost 500 years ago, when they finally caught certain sight of shore. Land birds and drifting wood had indicated for some time that land was nearby. Now, in the darkness, sailors were looking at light from far-off campfires. When dawn came, they made their way to the beach and soon were greeted by folk who brought them gifts of food, fresh water, and, as Columbus said in his journal, "whatever they had." The Europeans gazed upon the people they called "Indios" and Columbus described them as handsome, generous, and very peaceful. Within a day or so, he wrote of his intention to bring them into slavery.

In the days that followed, Columbus developed two themes in his depiction of the native peoples of the New World. One represented the Indians as beautiful and gentle people of childlike innocence. The other portrayed a popu-

lation he had not even met, but which he feared he would
encounter each time a strange cape was rounded or a new
island explored. According to the tales, there were people
here of unparalleled ferocity who gorged themselves on
human flesh. Coming from a war-torn and repressive
society, Columbus had no difficulty believing such tales, and
held himself and his forces in constant readiness.

From their earliest completely authenticated meeting,
the Europeans had conjured up these two contrasting
stereotypes of the Indians: noble children of nature and
savage devils. Through the centuries these two concepts
have helped devastate the relations between these two
populations, with the greatest damage being done, of
course, to the Native Americans. The first stereotype has
been associated with a policy of paternalism and patroniza-
tion, while the other has provided a rationale for massacres
and wholesale theft of Indian lands.

The point of raising such unpleasant subjects in this
introduction is to note happily that neither stereotype is
present in these pages, except as a subject of discussion, as in
Chapter 10. Instead, we see the Indians as they have been
and to some extent as they are at present, human beings who
developed a broad range of adaptive cultures. Like other
peoples the world over, they have had successes and failures.
Their worst reverses, however, have been suffered at the
hands of aliens from another continent, who forcibly took
over their world.

Indian populations have increased since the end of the
nineteenth century, when it seemed as if all peoples identi-
fied as Indians would become as extinct as their ancient
cultures. Unfortunately, the social problems that beset them
have also multiplied. These problems are mainly the legacy
of an early policy of virtual extermination by white people,
which has turned only rather recently into a less violent but
still malign discrimination. While references to the brutal
treatment suffered by Indians appear in various places in
this book, none is more graphic or poignant than the
retelling of the bitter story of Ishi (see Chapter 9).

But Paula Franklin's book is a celebration of the

richness and diversity of Indian culture as well as a commentary on its fate. The variety in Native American cultures is so great that the author showed her wisdom by limiting this book to the cultures that filled the area from the frozen tundra of the north to the arid sunlands this side of the Rio Grande. Perhaps in a second volume she may take us the rest of the way, to the region of Tierra del Fuego at the tip of South America. I hope for this because Paula Franklin's eye is keen and unsentimental, her grasp of the material sure, her prose fluent and interesting. Sticking to the facts as they have been assembled by anthropologists, historians, and a variety of writers, including Native Americans, she nonetheless speaks with a voice of friendship and sympathy. Since Wounded Knee is not yet behind us, we cannot be smug. We must know what Paula Franklin has to tell us.

1
WHO THEY ARE

When Christopher Columbus landed in America in 1492, he thought he had reached the part of Asia then known as the Indies, so he called the people he found living there "Indians." Columbus's term may have been a mistake, but at least it sounds better than "Skrellings," which is what the Vikings called the native peoples when they first encountered them around the year 1000. (Indians today are frequently called "Native Americans," although this term is not totally satisfactory either, since it is also used to describe everyone born in the United States.)

Misnamed or not, the newfound peoples across the Atlantic aroused the intense curiosity of Europeans, who wondered where they had come from. It seemed clear that they could not have originated in America, since the location of the Garden of Eden was presumed to have been in the eastern hemisphere. Some thought the Indians were related to the Ten Lost Tribes of Israel. Others believed they were descended from the Greeks. One early writer suggested that the Indians had traveled to the shores of America in "another Noes Arke."

As for the Indians themselves, most of them had no form of writing, and so they lacked written records to explain their history. The Maya Indians of Latin America did have a kind of writing, but we still don't know how to read most of it.

Beginning in the late 1800s, Indians (along with other peoples) were studied more scientifically by anthropologists and archeologists. They found ancient remains—human bones, artifacts, and the bones of animals—and learned to date them, at least approximately. As a result of their work, the Indian past is now generally thought to have happened more or less as follows:

Somewhere between 20,000 and 50,000 years ago, and possibly earlier, small groups of nomadic hunters began to migrate from Siberia to America. They were able to walk eastward in search of game because at that time the two continents of Asia and North America were joined by a land bridge across what is now Bering Strait.

These earliest Americans lived very simply. Apparently they had spears, tipped by stone points, and spear-throwers to help them throw the spears farther. They may have known how to tame dogs for help in hunting, and they probably knew how to make fire, which kept them warm and cooked their food.

Over the next several centuries, bands of hunters spread through North America, down across the Isthmus of Panama, and into South America. Their cultures became more complex as they invented the bow and arrow and a wide array of other specialized tools. They learned to farm, and so could settle down in one place instead of constantly moving. From a wild plant, they domesticated corn, which became the most important crop for all later Indians. Other native American plants grown by Indians were pumpkins and other kinds of squash, potatoes, beans, tomatoes, peppers, tobacco, and cotton.

Settled community life enabled the Indians to develop such complicated arts as basketry, pottery making, and weaving. Some groups created advanced cultures of great richness and power. The Aztec peoples, builders of cities and huge stone pyramids, ruled a large territory in Mexico. Farther south, the Maya—many of whose ceremonial centers still stand in the rain forests of Yucatán—developed a science of astronomy as well as a form of writing. In what is now Peru, the Inca empire, connected by a complex system of roads, stretched for hundreds of miles through the Andes.

By the time of European arrival in the fifteenth century, there were at least 8 million Indians in North and South America—perhaps as many as 75 million. All of them had changed their ways vastly from those of the simple hunters who had stumbled through the snow looking for game. Even the groups that still depended mainly on hunting—and there were many—had developed customs unknown to their ancestors.

Over the years, non-Indians have tended to develop a mental picture of the "typical Indian," who of course does not exist. For example, we think of "redskins," though Indians look less red than most whites or blacks. (The term may have been coined by early explorers who found Indians wearing red paint.) Indian skin color actually varies from white to a deep olive, and there is also a wide range in height and build. Physical features common to most Indians would include mainly straight black hair, sparse body hair, brown eyes, and prominent cheekbones.

In the matter of language, too, we tend to oversimplify the Indian reality. Movies have conditioned us to a limited vocabulary of grunts and broken English. But, before the coming of the whites, the Indians of North and South America spoke about 1,200 different languages. Many of these are related to one another and form what are known as *language families*. (The Romance language family, for example, consists of French, Spanish, Italian, Portuguese, and Romanian. These are languages with a common parent, Latin, and similar words and grammar.) North and South America, before the whites arrived, had about 160 language families, more native language families than all the rest of the world put together.

The distribution of Indian language families did not follow an obvious pattern. In some areas, all the Indians spoke related languages. In others, Indians only 20 miles apart might speak two totally different tongues, but both would be related to other languages hundreds of miles away.

Indian languages give us clues about the movement of Indian tribes before the coming of the whites. For example, some Indians in Canada speak a language closely related to that of the Navajo in the southwestern United States. This indicates that, sometime in the past, the two groups lived together, and that one (probably the Navajo) migrated outward.

Indians are often grouped according to tribe—such as the Cherokee, the Mohawk, the Apache. Before the whites arrived, there were 2,000 tribes in North America alone. In most cases, an Indian tribal name meant simply "the people" or "the real people." Indians—like the rest of us—were convinced that their own group was naturally superior, and that other people were inferior, or odd, or just plain stupid.

A tribe usually consisted of several small groups, either villages or wandering bands, that shared a language, a territory, and a way of life, or culture. Some tribes had a sense of group identity, of *being* a tribe. But most Indians did not have a strong tribal feeling, at least not until conflicts with the whites forced them to develop it. Among most Indians, there was no such thing as a single tribal chief. There were usually many chiefs, some for war and some for peace. Leadership changed hands along with a leader's achievements, or lack of them.

More important than the tribe were the individual band and the clan. A clan was made up of people who were related through a common ancestor. We might think of it as, say, the Brown family, except that descent (corresponding to the family name "Brown") often passed through the mother rather than the father. Because of this, a man might have considered himself more closely related to his sister's children than to his own.

The "typical Indian" of our imagination is usually decked out in a feather headdress and lives in a tipi. A few Indians did sport feather headdresses, but there was as much variety in Indian clothing as there is in a city today (probably more, since some Indians didn't wear anything at all). Indian shelters did include the pointed tipi made of

Subarctic

Hudson Bay

Northwest Coast

Pacific
Ocean

Woodlands

Plateau

Plains

Basin

Atlantic
Ocean

California

Southwest

Southeast

Gulf of Mexico

skins—but they also included the bark wigwam, the log-and-earth hogan, the adobe pueblo, and houses made of earth, planks, or grass.

Usually, Indians who lived near each other had the same way of life. For this reason it is easier to think in terms of just a few culture areas, rather than hundreds of different Indian languages or tribes. If you look at the map on page 5, you will see the location of the eight major culture areas of North America discussed in this book.

Sometimes people talk about "the Indian mind" or "the Indian soul." This is hard to describe because Indian life was so varied. But there are at least two characteristics that were probably universal among American Indians.

One was their attitude toward the land on which they lived. Indians did not believe in individual ownership. They didn't regard a garden plot or a mountain valley as belonging to one Indian or one family, to be passed down from generation to generation. Instead they thought of a given area as belonging to a group of people, usually a tribe, to be used by them in common. They held the same attitude toward food, especially if times were bad and people were hungry. If a hunter was lucky enough to kill an animal, it was understood that he would share it with everyone in the community.

The other common characteristic of Indians was their attitude toward the world around them, a feeling of union between people and their surroundings. In our "scientific" age, we have clear categories for animate (living) things, such as people, plants, and animals, and inanimate (nonliving) things, such as stones or wind. We also think of human beings as having speech and souls, while other beings have neither.

The Indian view was different. To Indians, the whole world was filled with supernatural force, and all things might display it or use it. For instance, Navajos would not say "I am hungry," but rather, "Hunger is killing me." They would say, not "I am drowning," but "Water is killing me." Indians believed that stones could move and a river could sing. Animals had souls and could even speak.

It was important for Indians, through control of their own spirits, to be in touch with the spirits around them. One old Indian described how children in his tribe were trained: "They were taught to use their organs of smell, to look when there was apparently nothing to see, and to listen intently when all seemingly was quiet. A child that cannot sit still is a half-developed child." If an Indian were lucky enough to acquire spiritual power (sometimes called good "medicine"), he or she could be protected from harm and even control the forces of nature. This is what we call magic. If a person used magic to harm innocent people, it became sorcery or witchcraft.

Because of their feelings about the world, Indians did not divide their lives into compartments the way we do. They did not draw sharp lines between work and play, between what was useful and what was beautiful, or between religious observances and everyday existence. All aspects of their culture flowed into each other. Indian life has been described as a conversation among beasts, trees, winds, stars, and man. Someone once said that, to an Indian, "The gods walk on every road of man, and every road of man is sacred."

2

PUEBLOS AND HOGANS

The Southwest

On a hot day in July, the townspeople were astir early. They had dressed in their best clothes and wore soft buckskin moccasins and jewelry of turquoise and silver. The men protected themselves from the heat with knotted head scarves or broad-brimmed hats. The women were dressed in dark wool blankets fastened over one shoulder. Both men and women had washed their hair in suds made from the yucca plant, as they did for all ceremonial occasions. Men wore their hair hanging straight, while married women had two simple braids. Unmarried girls were adorned with great circular rolls of hair on each side of the head—the "squash-blossom" hairdress.

Gradually people gathered in the open squares of the town. Some squatted in front of their houses. Others perched on the flat rooftops. Soon the sun would be baking the mesa, the high table of land on which their village stood.

Today was the last day of the Niman ceremony. For

eight days observances had been held inside the kivas, circular underground chambers reserved for the members of special religious organizations. There, men had made hundreds of prayer sticks. These short pieces of wood, carefully painted and decorated with bunches of colored feathers, would be "planted" before altars, in fields, and on hilltops to carry messages to the gods.

The members of one kiva conducted this year's Niman. Inside the kiva, the leader had made an altar of cloth, sacred objects, and designs of colored sand and cornmeal. Every morning for many days he had come to the kiva to chant the sixteen ritual songs that were part of Niman celebrations.

Now dancers were emerging from this kiva, moving slowly and with dignity. They would perform off and on all day, and there was no need for haste. All the dancers were men, though an outsider might not have known this, since everyone wore a mask. All were dressed alike, to represent the figure of Humis.

Humis was a kachina (*kuh*-CHEE-*nuh*). He was one of a group of supernatural beings who hovered among the people half the year and lived in the mountains the rest of the time. There were over 200 kachinas in all. Long ago, they had lived on earth, bringing rain and performing other useful services. But they had been massacred, leaving behind only their masks and costumes. After this catastrophe, the people donned the masks and costumes to dance and sing as the kachinas had taught them.

Now kachina dancers performed during the months when the kachinas were in their midst, beginning in the winter. At these special ceremonies the kachinas were thought to be actually present. The Niman festival (also known as the Home Dance) marked the return of the kachinas to their mountain home. They would not be back until December.

Like all the kachinas, Humis had his own special costume. He wore a high, painted wooden mask topped with eagle feathers. Since the mask completely covered his head, he peered out through two eye-slits. He wore blue armbands, a white embroidered kilt, and red moccasins. Small

The Humis kachina always wears spruce branches and a high wooden mask. Dancers might practice for as long as two months before the Niman festival.

spruce branches formed a collar below his mask, and larger ones hung down from the sash of his kilt. In his right hand he carried a gourd rattle. In his left hand he had still another sprig of spruce.

The dance began. Accompanied by drums and rattles, the kachina dancers, all dressed as Humis, sang as they circled the open square above the kiva. They called for rain to make the crops grow. Their steps were simple, repeated over and over again. The rhythmic tread of moccasined feet pounding across the hard-packed earth was thought to draw together the mist in the sky and heap it into rain clouds. There were no wild shouts, no frenzy, no high leaps or intricate steps—just a monotonous chant and the steady pounding of feet. The dance was a kind of dramatized prayer. Every step and gesture was part of an ancient ritual that had been handed down for centuries.

After a while the Humis dancers stopped for a rest and people relaxed. Then a second group of dancers emerged and took up a slightly different step. They too were all dressed alike, this time as Kachin-Mana, a female kachina. Again, all the dancers were men. Kachin-Mana's mask, topped by a single feather, had feather trimming around the neck. From the forehead, falling across the face, was an orange fringe, representing rainfall at dawn or sunset. Kachin-Mana wore the blanket and moccasins of an Indian maiden and a white shawl edged with red stripes.

And so the day passed. The dancers moved around the town, performing in all the main plazas. Every now and then they sat down to rest and gossip. Late in the afternoon, a special event occurred. All the young women who had been married in the past year came out in a group to watch the dancers. This was the first festival they had been allowed to watch. All four women, accompanied by older women sponsors, wore their white wedding blankets, woven for them by their husbands. Three of the sponsors carried infants that had been born to the "brides."

The highlight of the festival came at sunset. At that time, the kachina dancers presented boys with bows and arrows and gave little girls kachina dolls, small wooden copies of the kachina figures. These were given not only to please the children, but also to instruct them, so that over the years they would learn what each of the kachinas looked like. The kachina dancers passed out newly ripened corn and tender young melons and peaches to both boys and girls.

Finally a Hopi elder, called "the father of the kachinas," addressed a farewell speech to the dancers. The "father" then led the dancers down off the mesa to the west, where the kachinas' mountain home lay. Everyone in the village stood in silence until the dancers had disappeared from sight.

The Niman was one of the many ceremonies held every year by the Hopi Indians of the southwestern United States. The festival just described took place about seventy-five years ago. But the Niman was probably not very different five hundred years earlier. Before the coming of the whites, however, there would have been no silver jewelry, no woolen dresses, and no peaches or melons. (The Spaniards taught the Indians how to work silver, and brought sheep and many new foods to America.) Today Niman dances are still held, but they are briefer and have less meaning for the Hopi. Camera-clicking tourists crowd among the villagers, who sell them food and craftwork.

The Hopi are one group of Pueblo Indians, Indians who have lived in the southwestern United States for many centuries. The Pueblo people were the first Indians north of the Rio Grande to encounter whites, when Spaniards moved north from Mexico in the 1500s. And yet the Pueblo culture has changed less since contact with white people than that of any other group of North American Indians.

Several different groups of Indians have lived, and still live, in the Southwest. But the region is usually regarded as a single culture area. If you look at the map on page 5, you will see that the Southwest consists of New Mexico and Arizona plus southern Colorado and Utah, western Texas, and northwestern Mexico. Compared to other parts of America, this is not a very hospitable place to live. It is hot, and the average yearly rainfall is less than twenty inches. Much of the land is desert or semidesert. The country is high, with ranges of mountains and flat mesas rising from the level plateau. There may have been more rainfall at an earlier period, but it has never been a green and grassy land, at least not for some thousands of years.

The Southwest has an ancient history. Hunting peoples lived there at least 20,000 years ago. A later group apparently progressed beyond hunting for a livelihood. These were the Cochise people, who lived in Arizona and New Mexico. Diggers at Cochise sites have found large flattish stones with a hollow in them, indicating that the stones undoubtedly were used for grinding grain. Archeologists think that the Cochise people may have lived about 7,000 years ago. In the beginning they probably used the milling stones for grinding wild grains and nuts that they gathered. Later, Cochise people may also have done some farming, since agriculture in the Southwest seems to date back to at least 1000 B.C. Some say the first Southwest farmers may have been harvesting corn 6,000 years ago.

In spite of its climate, it is clear that the Southwest has been a farming region for centuries. It is the importance of farming, more than any other feature, that makes the Southwest a single culture area. Farming Indians have coped with the problem of drought in two chief ways. Either they have practiced dry farming, which means planting their crops in such a way as to take maximum advantage of the little rain that does fall, or they have dug irrigation canals and ditches to bring water to their crops from streams and rivers.

The earliest history of the Southwest is still shadowy. We do not know what happened to the early hunters or the Cochise people. But we do know a good deal about the Southwest of the last 2,000 years. In that period, it has been inhabited by three main groups of Indians: (1) the Anasazi; (2) other ancient villagers and their descendants; and (3) later, nomadic invaders.

The Anasazi people are probably the oldest inhabitants of the Southwest. The early Anasazi are known as the

Basketmaker people. Those of more recent times are called Pueblo. The word *Anasazi* is Navajo for "ancient ones." *Pueblo* means "village" in Spanish; the term is applied both to the towns and to their inhabitants.

Basketmaker culture probably developed before the birth of Christ. It flourished in the area around the San Juan River, where the present-day states of Utah, Colorado, Arizona, and New Mexico meet. This spot—the only place in the United States where four states come together—is known as the Four Corners. As their name indicates, the people are known for their fine baskets, some of which have been preserved for centuries in the dry air of the Southwest. They lived in caves and in huts made of adobe (sun-dried bricks of mud).

The first Basketmaker people farmed corn and squash, collected wild seeds, and captured small animals with nets and snares. Later these Indians clustered their huts in villages, learned how to make pottery and stone axes, and developed the bow and arrow.

Then, around 700 A.D., people began moving outward from the Four Corners. They also started growing cotton. But the most important single change in their way of life had to do with building. The earlier Anasazi had lived in small one-room huts. Now people began to construct many-roomed dwellings, which grew more and more elaborate.

The ruins of these first "apartment houses" still may be seen today. These pueblos were built with wooden frames covered by stone and adobe, and contained hundreds of rooms. Some had as many as five stories, each set back from the one below. Usually each family lived in a single room. This was not so confining as it seems to us, since, in the warm climate, people spent a good deal of time outdoors. Families that lived in upper stories had to climb up ladders and then down through a hole in the roof into their own room. Some rooms were used just for storage. Others, such as the kivas, were used for ceremonial purposes.

Probably the most famous of all these great pueblo dwellings are the ones in Mesa Verde National Park, in southwestern Colorado. Here the Indians built several

Cliff Palace in Mesa Verde National Park housed over 400 people when it was inhabited.

villages along ledges in the sides of canyons. (Because of these cliffside dwellings, some of the Anasazi people are called Cliff Dwellers.) The most spectacular of the Mesa Verde ruins is the "Cliff Palace," which has some 200 rooms arranged in four stories. The Indians who lived in cliff dwellings had to climb down the canyon walls to till their fields, which lay in valleys below.

Other well-known pueblos are in Chaco Canyon, in northern New Mexico. Here, too, early Indians, possibly "immigrants" from Mesa Verde, constructed a number of villages. There were twelve large ones and many smaller ones. Pueblo Bonito, on the floor of the canyon, was shaped like a big "D." The curved side consisted of a great semicircle of clustered rooms, rising to five stories. Along the straight side was a wall of single rooms. Pueblo Bonito covered three acres and, with 800 rooms, was probably home for at least 1,200 inhabitants. It was considered to be the largest apartment house in the world until a larger one was built in New York City in the 1880s.

There are some mysteries about these pueblos. One mystery is why they were built in the first place. Some people think the purpose was defensive. Certainly the big structures were well protected against animals and hostile tribes. But archeologists have found few signs of violence around pueblo sites. Also, it is known that some Indians of the time continued to live in isolated single-family houses, so the danger could not have been very great. The buildings were apparently added to many times over the years. Did constant building activity provide an outlet for energy and aggression, which could not otherwise be expressed in these Indians' well-ordered lives?

Another mystery is why the great pueblos were abandoned. This seems to have happened sometime between 1275 and 1300 A.D. Some people think that the Pueblo people were threatened by hostile outsiders; it was around this time that nomadic invaders moved into the region from farther north. Again, though, the few signs of violence seem to contradict this theory. Besides, the location and organization of the Pueblo people should have given them the advantage over their opponents. Maybe a long dry spell forced the Indians to move. Archeologists know that there was a dry period in the late 1200s because tree rings from this time are much narrower than those before and after—a sure sign of drought.

At any rate, the great "apartment houses," once alive with the hum of activity, fell deserted and silent. Their inhabitants moved away to the south. There they built smaller, simpler villages of stone and adobe—the pueblos found by the Spaniards in the 1500s. Actually, some of these Pueblo people began to build such villages even earlier. Two of them, Oraibi in Arizona and Acoma in New Mexico, were founded about a thousand years ago. They claim to be the oldest continuously inhabited towns in the United States.

The three chief Pueblo areas have been for some time (1) Hopi land, with several villages, including Oraibi, on three mesas in northeastern Arizona; (2) Zuñi, a pueblo about a hundred miles east, just across the New Mexico border; and (3) eighteen pueblos, including Acoma, along the Rio Grande in north-central New Mexico.

In spite of their common past, the Pueblo Indians do not share a common language. The Hopi have their own language, related to that of some other non-Pueblo Indians in the area. The Zuñi language is unique, and the Rio Grande pueblos are divided into two other language groups.

Throughout most of their history, the Pueblo Indians' way of life did not change very much. The people were farmers and lived in close-knit, permanent village communities. They were extremely peaceful and usually fought only when attacked. There was no honored place in their society for warriors or for people who wanted to compete with their fellow citizens for prestige.

Every aspect of life—government, hunting, warfare (when it was necessary), weather "control"—was under the charge of a specific group, a society of men. The elders in each society were really priests. They knew the proper rituals for planting, seeking rain, averting storms, curing illness, and defending the village. They ruled the societies and, in effect, the village.

Pueblo life revolved around a definite "calendar of events." Each fixed ceremony had its own ritual and purpose, though most involved an attempt to bring rain for the crops. Pueblo people felt vitally concerned about the details of these occasions: how well they were carried out, who wore a new costume, who had composed a new song. Personal matters such as births, marriages, and deaths were less important. One of the highest Pueblo ideals was proper discipline and correct behavior in carrying out the rituals without a mistake.

Most Pueblo Indians worshiped a Mother Earth and a Father Sky. There were also war gods, who were feared. The most-loved supernatural beings were the kachinas, who were regarded as messengers between gods and humans. Each village had at least one kachina cult. Some had as many as six, just as small American towns may have six different Protestant churches.

Every man in a Pueblo village belonged to at least one kachina cult. Boys were initiated at about the age of twelve. Before that time, children were supposed to believe that the kachina dancers *were* the kachinas themselves. Adults encouraged the belief, in somewhat the same way that people teach children about Santa Claus and the Easter Bunny today. One Hopi has described how, when he was a boy, kachinas came into the village, bringing bean sprouts in their baskets.

> We were in the plaza watching them. Suddenly my mother threw a blanket over my head. When she uncovered me the kachinas were all gone and the people were looking up in the sky and watching them fly about— they said. I looked up but could see nothing. My mother laughed and said that I must be blind.[1]

When boys joined a cult, they were told the truth about the dancers and instructed in kachina lore. Women could belong to kachina cults, too. This happened in one of two ways. If they were cured by kachina-cult rituals, they had to join the cult, since only its members could possess the sacred knowledge of curing illness. And membership was also required if anyone mistakenly entered a kiva while a ceremony was in progress.

Members of a kachina cult were responsible for making masks, fashioning kachina dolls for the little girls, and conducting the kachina dances held during the six months of each year when the kachinas were "in residence." The Indians took their responsibilities seriously. If dancers were not pure of heart, they would be punished by the kachinas. So, as they put on their masks, dancers would plead, "Please do not cause me any serious trouble."

Absorbed in the rituals of planting and harvesting, the Pueblo lived in relative peace and security for over 200 years. Then, in 1539, they were visited by strangers from the south. In that year a Spanish friar, Fray Marcos de Niza, and his black companion, Estevanico, got as far as Zuñi before Estevanico was killed. The friar hurried back to Mexico with excited stories about the "seven cities of Cíbola" full of gold. (There were then seven Zuñi villages.) Naturally, his report aroused greedy adventurers. The next year Francisco de Coronado led an exploring party north from Mexico, but he found no gold. He massacred many Pueblo people out of frustration and then returned home.

For the next several decades, the Indians were left alone. Then more Spaniards came in the late 1590s. They founded the town of Santa Fe in 1610. From the Indians' point of view, nothing very good came of this. The Indians did learn to raise sheep and cattle, to weave wool, to work metal, to grow wheat, and to grow fruit trees. Some adopted Christianity. But, regarded as little better than slaves, they were exploited and weakened by disease. There had been some eighty Pueblo villages when the Spaniards first came. As time went by, over half of these villages were abandoned.

In 1680 the Pueblo people revolted. They were led by Popé, an old man from the Rio Grande pueblo of San Juan. Carefully organized and advised through a network of runners carrying news of when to attack, the Indians rose up and drove the whites out of their territory and even out of Santa Fe. Their hard-won independence lasted just twelve years. The Spaniards succeeded in sowing suspicion among the pueblos, pitted various groups against each other, and so were able to win the territory back.

In the years that followed, Pueblo villages dwindled to their present number. Outside rulers came and went. The Spanish were followed in 1821 by the Mexicans. Americans took over after winning the Mexican War in 1848. But Pueblo ways continued much as before, as you will read in the last chapter.

The second major Southwest group after the Anasazi is a "family" of ancient village dwellers and their descendants. They are not closely related, but they have several features in common.

One ancient culture is called Hohokam, from an Indian word meaning "those who have vanished." The Hohokam people lived in south-central Arizona, south of where Phoenix stands today. They flourished from around the time of Christ to about 1400 A.D. In this very dry area, the Indians solved their farming problems by building great irrigation channels, 10 feet deep and up to 30 feet wide. In the valley of the Salt River alone, there were 150 miles of irrigation channels. Hohokam people lived in earth lodges. Working cooperatively, they carried out their digging projects with the simplest wood and stone tools.

Another early Southwest people were the Mogollon. They lived along the Gila River in eastern Arizona and western New Mexico. They may have been related to the Hohokam, though they did not practice irrigation. Both people apparently lived at about the same time.

The Mogollon people are best known for their pottery, which is considered some of the most beautiful and interesting ever made. It is called Mimbres pottery, since most of it has been found in the valley of the Mimbres River. The Mogollon people lavished tremendous care on their bowls and jars. They were masterful painters. One bowl has twenty-seven parallel lines painted across the width of a band less than two inches wide. Much of the pottery has survived because it was buried with its makers. Each buried

*This Mimbres bowl is probably at least 700 years old. A large bird—
its body pierced by a hole—grasps a rabbit in its beak.*

vessel has a hole pierced in it. This ceremonial "killing" of pottery released the "spirit" of the vessel, which was thought to be a part of its maker's soul.

Both older groups, Hohokam and Mogollon, somehow lost their early vigor, and a number of different tribes grew up in their place. The Pima and Papago of Arizona were probably descendants of the Hohokam people. One similarity the Pima had with the Hohokam was the irrigation system. Other small groups of the Southwest, possibly related to the Hohokam or Mogollon, were the Yuma and the Mohave.

Most of these Indians lived in little brush houses. They did some farming, but depended heavily on wild animals and plants for food. They were more warlike than the Pueblo, less settled, and less devoted to rituals.

The third major Southwest Indian "family" consists of two groups of nomadic hunters who invaded the Pueblo region from the north sometime after 1200 A.D. Their languages are similar to each other, very different from those of the Southwest but related to Indian languages spoken in Canada and Alaska. To us, the two groups seem very unlike, but a long time ago they were one. The Southwest residents whose territory they invaded named them *apachu* ("enemies") and *apachu de nabahu* ("enemies of the cultivated fields")—to use our English words, Apache and Navajo. Clearly, they were a threat to the peaceful villagers who had tilled their cornfields for generations.

After entering the Southwest, if not before, the two groups of northern invaders separated. The Apache lived as nomadic hunters. They ranged up and down the countryside and preyed on the settled villages in their path.

The Apache were tough and ferocious. They began to use horses in the 1600s, when some were stolen or escaped from Spanish settlements. After that, the Apache became more of a threat than ever. Young men were trained in the arts of war by dodging arrows shot at them by fellow tribesmen. They learned to endure the brutal heat of the Southwest by running for miles in the hot sun with a

Navajo weaving is highly prized all over the world. Many people on the Navajo reservation still live in hogans like the one shown at right.

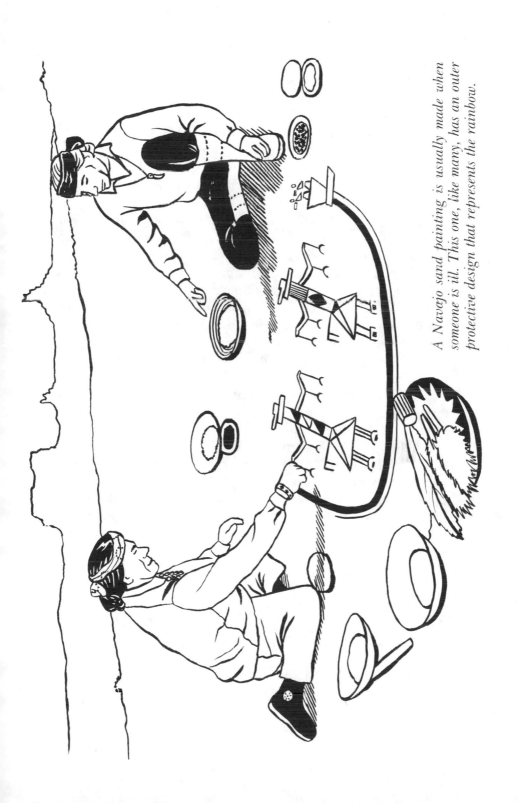

A Navajo sand painting is usually made when someone is ill. This one, like many, has an outer protective design that represents the rainbow.

mouthful of water, only to spit it out at the end of the course to show their disdain for a cooling drink. Enemies were treated without mercy, sometimes taken out in the desert sun to be devoured by animals.

The Apache kinsfolk, the Navajo, reacted differently to the new land in which they found themselves. While the Apache stole from the Pueblo people in plundering raids, the Navajo "stole" from them by imitating their culture, sometimes becoming more accomplished at Pueblo skills than the Pueblo themselves.

The Navajo built their earth-and-wood hogans near Pueblo villages. They came into especially close contact with the older Southwesterners when some Pueblo took refuge with them after the 1680 revolt against the Spaniards. From the Pueblo Indians the Navajo learned to farm, herd sheep, and weave wool. Their weaving eventually excelled that of the Pueblo people. The Pueblo had long made "paintings" out of colored sand to adorn the altars of their kivas. The Navajo developed sand painting to its highest point. Priests made handsome designs for healing ceremonies, creating and destroying them on the same day. The Navajo grew to love their adopted land, and to pray for rain with the same intensity as the Pueblo people.

When the Americans won the Southwest in 1848, they tried to get the Apache to settle on small reservations and take up farming. Some did settle down, but others kept moving about, plundering both Indian and white settlements for food, horses, and weapons. The simple brush wickiups in which they lived could be dismantled and made ready to move in an hour.

One band in particular, the Chiricahua Apache, terrorized settlements in southern Arizona, New Mexico, and northern Mexico, retreating up into the hills where no one dared follow them. Though they, too, were bundled onto a reservation in the late 1800s, life there did not satisfy them. Under a strong warrior, Geronimo, a number of families escaped. Then a sort of duel began, with a few hundred Apache raiding settlements and eluding the United States Army for over twenty years. Geronimo finally surrendered

Geronimo

in 1886, but his people were held as prisoners of war until 1913.

All was not peace and quiet with the Navajo, either. They were enough like the Apache to become restless with a completely settled routine. In the 1700s they had begun to acquire quantities of horses and sheep. Their settlements spread out over large areas of Arizona and New Mexico, completely surrounding the Hopi and Zuñi. Soon the Navajo were living pretty much as they pleased, forcing other Indians to do their hard work, while they bragged about their flocks and turned out ever more beautiful craftwork.

After 1848, Americans were faced with "the Navajo problem." As with other tribes, they signed peace treaties with the Navajo and allotted them land. But the Indians regarded the treaties as meaningless scraps of paper, which they agreed to in order to receive gifts of food and cloth goods. They went on raiding as before. Finally, in 1864, the frontier scout Kit Carson was assigned the task of rounding up the Navajo and subduing them. His solution was to starve them out by killing their sheep and destroying their fields.

The Navajo were told that the federal government would feed and care for them at Bosque Redondo, near Fort Sumner in eastern New Mexico. So 7,000 Navajo, dejected and half starved, gave up. There they lived for four years, unhappy and dreaming of their homeland to the west. In 1868, the United States signed a final peace treaty with the Navajo, allowing them a reservation near Four Corners and giving them small allotments of sheep and goats. The last chapter describes what reservation life meant for them.

3

MOUNDS AND THEIR MAKERS

The Southeast

Near the end of the Revolutionary War, a Virginia gentleman decided it was time to do something about a big hill that
stood near his home. Everyone agreed that it was no
ordinary hill, but had been constructed by human hands.
There were many such "barrows"—as they were called
then—in this pleasant countryside. And people wondered
how they had been built. The Virginian wrote:

> The barrows are to be found all over this region. These
> are of different sizes, some built of earth and some of
> loose stones. It was obvious that they were burial places,
> but no one was sure how they had been constructed.
> Some thought they covered the bones of those who fell in
> battles that were fought at these spots. Others believed
> they contained the bones of many Indians, collected at
> certain periods and deposited in one place. Still others

thought they were town graveyards. According to one
Indian tradition, when they settled in a town, the first
person who died was placed standing up and earth was
placed around the body to cover and support it. When
another person died, a narrow passage was dug to the
first, the second leaned against the first body, the cover of
earth replaced, and so on. I wanted to find out whether
any of these opinions was right, and decided to open a
mound and examine it thoroughly.[1]

The curious investigator went about his task in a systematic
way:

I first dug in several parts of it, and came to collections of
human bones, at different depths, from six inches to
three feet below the surface. These were lying in great
confusion, some upright, some flat, and pointing in every
which way. Bones of the most distant parts were found
together—for instance, the small bones of the foot in the
hollow of a skull. There were some teeth which I judged
to be smaller than those of an adult; a skull which
appeared to be that of an infant; a rib and a fragment of
jaw of a person about half grown; another rib of an
infant; a part of the jaw of a child which had not cut its
teeth.
   I then made a cut through the mound, wide enough
for a man to walk through and examine its sides. At the
bottom I found bones; above these a few stones, then a
large interval of earth, then a layer of bones, and so on.
The bones nearest the surface were least decayed. No
holes were discovered in any of them, as if made with
bullets, arrows, or other weapons. I guessed that this
barrow might have a thousand skeletons.[2]

After making his discoveries, the writer reached these
conclusions:

It is easy to see that this mound did not cover only the
bones of persons fallen in battle, and that the bodies were
not placed upright touching each other. Instead it was a
collection of bones that had been placed together. The

first collection had been deposited on the surface of the earth, a few stones put over it, and then a covering of earth. The second had been laid on this, and so on.[3]

The Virginia gentleman who carried out this investigation was Thomas Jefferson. Mounds like the one he excavated, and many much larger and more elaborate, were found throughout a large area of the United States. This region stretched from Pennsylvania to Missouri, as far north as Wisconsin and as far south as Florida.

It was natural that Jefferson, a man of wide-ranging intelligence, should be interested in everything around him. He was not only a great leader and political writer, but also an architect, an inventor, and a scientist. He collected fossils and studied the birds of his native Virginia. He also compiled vocabularies of Indian languages. (In 1791 he traveled with James Madison to Long Island to jot down word lists from three old women.)

But, while Jefferson's thoroughness and logic were natural for him, they were unusual for his time. The science of archeology did not exist yet. Since the deserted mounds contained handsome art objects as well as bones, it was obvious that whoever built them had had a complex way of life. The Indians who now lived nearby, and who had a relatively simple culture, seemed to know nothing about the mounds. Therefore, many people thought, the mounds had been built by some mysterious race that had vanished centuries earlier, the "Mound Builders." Many scholars were convinced that the builders of the mounds were descendants of the Ten Lost Tribes of Israel. A woman poet, however, believed that they were Phoenicians from the ancient Mediterranean city of Tyre. And, according to another theory, the mounds were Viking tombs.

Still, there were always a few people (including Jefferson) who believed that the mounds had been built by Indians. Time and careful investigations proved that they were right. The history of these Indians has been pieced together, even though many gaps still remain.

The oldest group of mound-building Indians were the

Adena people, named after remains found near Chillicothe, Ohio. They lived in the valley of the Ohio River, in Pennsylvania, Ohio, Indiana, Kentucky, and West Virginia. They may well have been the first people in eastern North America to farm, since they grew corn, tobacco, and gourds at an early date. Just how early is not known, though one site in Kentucky apparently goes back to 700 B.C. Other places seem to have been settled as late as the 700s A.D.

The Adena people were the first Indians in what is now the United States to build large earthen mounds. Some of these mounds are as high as 70 feet. Bodies were buried inside, usually along with stone pipes and ornaments of copper, shell, and mica. It is possible that each mound was built for a single chief, and that the other bodies buried in it are those of wives and servants who were killed when he died.

Another group of mound builders are called the Hopewell people, named after a mound in Ross County, Ohio. They left remains all the way from Missouri to the Florida coast. Their most important sites are in southern Ohio and in the valleys of the Illinois and Mississippi rivers in Illinois. No one is sure when this culture flourished. It may have existed at about the same time as Adena, though it was probably later.

Hopewell mounds are larger and more elaborate than

Hopewell mounds are noted for their stone pipe sculptures. This one shows a hawk or eagle attacking a man.

Adena mounds. They are often surrounded by miles of earthen walls. The objects found inside with the burials are of great beauty and superb workmanship. They include carved pipes, pearl necklaces, birds and fish made of beaten copper, and thin sheets of mica in the form of hands, claws, and human figures. There are also blades made from the volcanic glass known as obsidian. These Indians must have traded far and wide. The obsidian they used is found in Yellowstone National Park, and the copper comes from the Lake Superior region. The Hopewell people were the finest Indian metalworkers in North America.

A third group of mound-building Indians, the Mississippians, probably lived between 1000 and 1600 A.D. The mounds they built served as bases for temples. These were part of huge ceremonial centers, with open plazas. The Mississippian people lived mainly in the southern United States, from Georgia west to the Mississippi River, and north as far as Illinois.

One great site of this period is the Cahokia Mounds near East St. Louis, Illinois. One of the mounds there, Monks Mound, measures roughly 100 feet high, 1,000 feet long, and 700 feet wide. Covering an area of 16 acres, it is considered the largest single man-made earthen structure in the world.

Mississippian people also built at a site called Etowah, near Carterville, Georgia. Here their village extended 3,000 feet along the Etowah River and 1,500 feet inland, with a moat to protect the area away from the river. There were several temple mounds. The largest was about 70 feet high and 380 feet square at the base. This mound probably contained well over 4 million cubic feet of earth.

Some Indians built still another kind of mound. This was the effigy mound in the shape of a living creature, almost always an animal. Most effigy mounds are in southern Wisconsin and in nearby areas of Illinois and Iowa, although Ohio has some, too. All kinds of animals are represented. There are bears, deer, panthers, wolves, turtles, and birds. The mounds are low but of great size. For example, one mound in the shape of a bird is 6 feet high but

Because it is so low, Ohio's Great Serpent Mound is best seen from the air.

has a wingspread of 624 feet. And the Great Serpent Mound in Ohio, only 2 feet in height, spreads its coils out to cover over 1,000 feet. Sometimes bodies were buried in the effigy mounds, at the location of the brain or heart. No one really knows when they were constructed, or by whom.

At least two things can be deduced about the mound-building Indians. One is that they must have had advanced cultures. They were not nomadic hunters, but farmers, and they made quite beautiful art objects. They probably lived and worked together in well-organized communities. It took cooperation and a long time to build the huge earthen mounds, which were piled together completely by hand, without even the use of a wheelbarrow.

The other deduction is this: There must have been some sort of contact between eastern North America and Mexico. The Maya and Aztec Indians constructed very elaborate pyramids around open plazas. Their houses were also like those of the mound builders, and so were many of their artistic techniques.

Most of the Indians who lived around the Gulf of Mexico had canoes, so travel back and forth would not have been hard. Probably the mound builders learned from Mexican Indians who traveled north to trade or hunt and then returned home.

It is not known why the Indians of the eastern United States stopped building mounds. But, whatever the reason, these people didn't vanish mysteriously. Gradually taking on simpler ways, they developed into the various groups white people first encountered around the Gulf of Mexico and the southern Atlantic coast in the 1600s.

The Southeast culture area is somewhat larger than that of the Southwest. It consists of the southeastern United States from southern Virginia and West Virginia across the Mississippi and into eastern Texas. The climate is mild, the region is thickly forested and well watered with streams. Centuries ago, it was full of wild game.

The first southeastern Indians with whom the whites became familiar were the Natchez, who lived near the city in Mississippi that is named for them. The French controlled this area in the late 1600s and have left many accounts of the Indians they found there.

The Natchez seem to have been almost the only Indians in the United States that did not have a democratic form of government. They were governed by an absolute ruler known as the Sun, who was regarded as the brother of the sun in the sky. "This grand chief," wrote one Frenchman, "is as absolute as a king. His people do not come near him through respect. When they speak to him, they are four paces distant. Only his wife can eat at his table. When he gives the leftovers to his brothers or any of his relatives, he pushes the dishes to them with his feet. On rising, all the relatives approach his bed, and raising their arms on high, make frightful cries. They salute him thus without his paying any attention."[4]

The Natchez Sun wore only the finest garments and was carried in a litter so that his feet would not have to touch the ground. His people supported him and his family with gifts of food and game. The Natchez system of social classes was a complicated one, with three groups of nobles and a class of commoners known as Stinkards. The French, who gave them this name, said that they were only translating the Indian term. (But they did note that none of the people in this class liked to hear the word.)

When the French first observed the Natchez, they were still building mounds in the seven villages in which they lived. True, the mounds were only a few feet high, with simple huts made of poles and thatch built on top of them. But they clearly seem to have been the "descendants" of the big earth structures built years earlier. Most of the huts were temples, but one was the home of the Great Sun himself. Each morning, wrote another French observer, "the great chief honors by his presence the rising of his elder brother [the sun], and salutes him with many howlings as soon as he appears above the horizon. Afterward he raises his hand above his head and, turning from the east to the west, he shows him the direction which he must take in his course."[5]

The Natchez farmed, hunted, and, above all, fought. In the early 1700s, they warred so much with neighboring tribes that they were all but wiped out. Though the Natchez perished or were absorbed by neighboring Indians, many of their customs are reflected among other groups of the region, such as the Mobile, Tunica, and Biloxi. Other Indians of the Southeast included the Tuscarora, Timucua, Yuchi, Creek, Choctaw, Chickasaw, and Cherokee. According to Creek tradition, their people came into the Southeast when the region was already settled, and this may have been true for the Chickasaw and Choctaw, too. Although the political organization of these Indians was more democratic than that of the Natchez, they had many other features in common.

Southeastern Indians dressed simply, but they liked tattoos and shell jewelry. The open-sided shelter on stilts was common among the Seminole people.

One was their appearance. Since the Southeast has a warm climate, the Indians dressed accordingly. There was no need for heavy clothing, or even moccasins. A woman usually wore little more than a simple wraparound skirt made of buckskin or bark fiber, with maybe a few strings of shell beads. A man wore a breechcloth, a strip of buckskin or cloth that he passed between his legs and fastened in front and back by lapping it over a belt.

Southeastern men were proud of their appearance. If they had won honors in warfare, they were heavily tattooed. After each successful exploit, a warrior was allowed to "record" it on his body in the form of a design. This was done by scratching the skin with a sharp fish's tooth and rubbing in soot from the fire. Dressed for a ceremony, a warrior might wear shell or copper earrings and a robe made of fur or feathers.

A brave plucked out most of the hair on his head with clamshell tweezers, leaving only a scalplock to dare his enemies to come after him. In the Southeast, as through most of North America, a scalp was a trophy, just as an enemy pistol or flag is today. Stretched and dried, it decorated the warrior's lance and showed everybody what he had done. Scalping was not necessarily fatal, and many people who were scalped lived to tell about it.

Southeastern Indians were farmers. Both men and women worked in the fields, raising corn, beans, and squash. Their farms were not very big because game and fish were plentiful, and wild berries and roots were abundant in the forest. People lived in small villages. They built houses of wood and reeds plastered together with mud and covered with thatch. These surrounded a central square, where there stood a temple (often on a mound), the chief's house, and a council house.

Most southeasterners, even if they were not as tightly organized as the Natchez, had a well-run system of government. Each town was more or less independent. The chief, called a *mico* by the Creek (and "king" by the English), wore a feather cloak and was carried on a litter. He was advised on village matters by a council of retired warriors known as the Beloved Men.

In times of trouble with other settlements, another chief, Big Warrior, took command. By beating on a drum, he organized a war party of young men. They met in his house and fasted for three days, drinking the "Black Drink" to cleanse themselves. This was made from the ilex plant, and induced vomiting almost as soon as it was swallowed. The "Black Drink" was valued throughout the Southeast as a purifying agent. It was used on many religious occasions, and preparing for war was one of these.

Warfare to the southeasterners, as to most Indians, was part game, part ritual, part status-seeking—and all-important. It was the only way a young southeastern man could prove himself. Until a youth had gone on a war party, he was called by a "baby name" and regarded as a child. From infancy, a boy was taught the arts of war and to admire the bravery and self-discipline of a warrior. Any boy who was afraid to face battle, or who showed cowardice in actual combat, had to wear women's clothes and live as a woman the rest of his life.

While the young men fasted in Big Warrior's house, they staged dances and songs, describing in vivid detail how they would defeat the enemy. When they were ready to depart, they painted themselves for magical protection. They carried only a few handfuls of dried corn to live on. Creeping silently through the forest, they sometimes walked in each other's footsteps so that an enemy would not realize how many warriors there were. There were hardly ever more than thirty or forty.

Indian warfare in North America—before the coming of the whites, anyway—was rarely warfare on a large scale. No big armies set forth. Instead there were commando raids. Men would suddenly swoop down on a village, throw firebrands on thatched roofs, and club and scalp people as they ran out of their homes.

Sometimes the southeasterners killed for vengeance, to pay back a wrong. Sometimes they killed for the prestige of

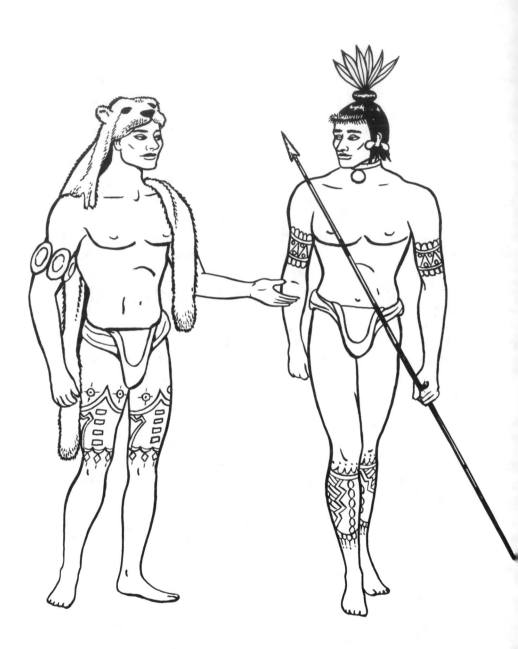

The tattoos and headdresses of warriors were symbols of their achievements, like a modern soldier's medals and ribbons. Hair drawn into a topknot, like that of the Indian on the right, was typical among the Timucua, who lived in northern Florida.

it, carrying back scalps, or an arm or leg, to bear witness to their bravery. Often they fought to obtain captives.

Upon returning from a raid, any member of the war party who had killed someone had to undergo purification, secluding himself and fasting and praying. This was a precaution thought to keep away the ghosts of enemies who had been slain.

Women and children captives were usually adopted into the village. So were young men, especially if a family had recently lost its breadwinner. But a wounded warrior, who would not be able to earn his keep, or a seasoned fighter, whose many tattoos testified to his prowess, was reserved for torture.

About three days after a raid, villagers gathered around the public square for the spectacle. The prisoner was tied to a stake and slowly tortured to death, usually with torches and knives. The captive was supposed to enter into the spirit of the event, taunting his attackers and singing songs of courage. Women took the lead in prolonging the captive's agony. They revived him when he fainted, and sometimes let him rest so that the spectacle could last a long time.

This kind of torture was common in much of the eastern United States. It is hard for us to understand, because Indians took pleasure in their victims' pain. Of course this was a cruel age in "civilized" Europe, too, when crowds gathered in public squares to watch heretics being burned alive at the stake. It may be that torturing started as a way in which women could relieve their grief over their husbands, sons, and brothers who had been killed. Then— just as the ancient Romans came to love their bloody spectacles, when gladiators fought each other to the death— the people began to enjoy the experience and made it more and more cruel.

To the southeasterners, fighting was one of the most important occupations a man could have. The British once suggested to the Cherokee that they make peace with a neighboring tribe. The Cherokee answered that if they did so, they would just have to find someone else to fight, since "We cannot live without war."

When southeastern warriors died, their souls were thought to travel along the Milky Way to a sort of happy hunting ground. The whites, who liked this idea, applied it to most of the Indians they encountered. Actually, however, most Indians had only the vaguest idea of an afterlife. They were concerned mainly with proper disposal of the dead in order to avoid being haunted by their spirits.

Like medieval knights with their tournaments, the southeasterners sometimes substituted games for war. In fact, the Cherokee called games "the little brother of war." The southeasterners were especially fond of chunkey, their form of the Indian game the French named lacrosse. They played it with netted rackets and a hair-stuffed ball. Sometimes the blows inflicted on opposing players were severe enough to cause death.

The southeasterners, like most Indians, believed that everything in the world was inhabited by a spirit force. They thought that people had to learn how to cope with this force as it showed itself in animals, plants, and natural happenings such as rain and wind. The Creek believed that each animal controlled some ailment that it could cause or cure, depending on the kind of treatment the animal received. The Cherokee had a neat solution to this problem. According to them, animals sent disease in revenge for being killed by humans. But plants, being merciful, provided remedies.

Two special groups were called upon to help ordinary people in their dealings with the supernatural. One group was the priests, who were always men. They knew all the lore of prayers and rituals, what kind of dance brought rain, and what kind of body paint brought success in battle. The other group was the shamans, often called "medicine men" by whites—although women could be shamans, too. While the priests learned what they knew only after long study, the shamans' magic power came directly from the spirit-world in a dream or vision. They could use this power for good or ill, curing disease or using "black magic" to harm their enemies.

The most important ceremonial occasion for the Southeast Indians was the busk (this word is the white people's version of the Indian *boskita,* meaning "to fast"). It was

celebrated once a year when the corn first ripened, sometime in July or August. It was a kind of New Year's
celebration, when people turned over a new leaf. Women
put out their household fires, cleaned their homes thoroughly, and tossed away old dishes and worn-out clothing.
New tools and weapons were made. All sins were forgiven,
except murder. In the town plaza, the men prayed and
fasted, and a new fire was kindled from which people started
new fires in their homes. After this, everyone feasted on
young corn, danced, and played chunkey and gambling
games.

Like the Indians of the Southwest, the Southeast Indians had a long heritage. And like the southwesterners, they
were among the first Indians north of the Rio Grande to
come into contact with the whites. De Soto went through
their territory in the 1540s when he marched from Florida
to the Mississippi River. After the Spanish founded St.
Augustine (Florida) in 1565, missionaries converted many of
the nearby Indians to Christianity. In the late 1600s, the
French began to set up posts along the coast of the Gulf of
Mexico. Meanwhile the English were establishing themselves
along the Atlantic coast to the north.

Luckily for the Indians of the Southeast, it was quite a
while before whites actually wanted to settle in their territory. Instead, Spain, France, and England each tried to win
the allegiance of the Indians in order to strengthen itself
against its rivals. For a long time this policy worked in favor
of the Indians, or at least the stronger tribes. With threats
and promises, they cleverly manipulated the whites in order
to gain land, metal tools, and guns. Less cleverly, they let the
whites play upon their own rivalries and so diminish their
numbers. For instance, the English helped supply the Creek
with weapons and goaded them on to destroy the Chris-
tianized Indians of Florida.

One group of Creek, who did not care for this inter-
ference by white people, fled their homeland and retreated
into the Florida swamps. Thus they were given the name
Seminole, the Creek word for "runaway."

As time went on, rivalry between the French and the English became more and more bitter. A series of four wars ended in 1763, with the English dominant in North America. The Creek had allied themselves with the English and had established a widespread confederacy of tribes. But their heyday lasted only about twenty years. By then the American colonists had fought and won the Revolutionary War, gained their independence, and forced the English out.

Now the Indians began to realize that the whites were not weak strangers who could be tossed about like chunkey balls. Indeed, they were strong, both in numbers and in weapons. And now they wanted Indian land. A great Shawnee leader, Tecumseh, traveled down from the north in 1811 and 1812 to rally Indians against the whites. He found willing listeners in the Southeast, but he failed in his long-range plan to unite all the eastern tribes into one fighting force. Nevertheless, his powerful speeches stirred some of the Creek, who "went on the warpath" against the whites in 1813.

The resulting Creek War was not so much a war as a series of skirmishes. Each side launched raids and massacres. Andrew Jackson led one force of American frontiersmen, who were helped by friendly Creek and by Choctaw. A final and decisive encounter took place in March 1814, when Jackson and 2,000 men defeated a large Creek army at the Horseshoe Bend of the Tallapoosa River in Alabama. The Creek had to sign a treaty handing over southern Alabama and Georgia.

Farther east, the Seminole of Florida also put up a fight against the whites. In the First Seminole War, fought from 1816 to 1818, they met the same fate as their Creek cousins—defeat at the hands of Andrew Jackson. Florida, up to now a Spanish possession, became part of the United States.

After this, most of the Southeast Indians, seeing that they were helpless against the whites, decided that the best thing to do was to adopt white customs. In just a few years, they settled down and took up farming in earnest, becoming as peaceful and law-abiding as the meekest of Pennsylvania Quakers. The Creek, Choctaw, Chickasaw, Cherokee, and Seminole were often called the Five Civilized Tribes.

These Indians were quite good at civilized ways. A Cherokee named Sequoyah taught himself how to read and write the "talking leaves," through which the Americans communicated in English. Then he developed a special kind of alphabet for the Cherokee language. Soon almost every member of the tribe knew how to read and write Cherokee. It is said that young people sometimes went on trips just so they could show off by writing letters home to their friends.

In the long run, the Indians' efforts to adapt to white ways proved useless. In 1830 the United States government changed its Indian policy. Previously it had left Indians to fend for themselves after buying their land. Now the government decided to move them into a specially designated area (later to become the state of Oklahoma). At the time, this land west of the Mississippi was thought to be worthless for white settlement.

Among the first Indians to be affected by the new Indian Removal Act were the southeasterners. Their protests did no good. Family after family had to sell their farms and most of their belongings. They were forced to accept ridiculously low payments, since the whites knew that the Indians had no choice but to take whatever they could get.

Thousands of Indians were herded westward by United States troops. Often the pace was brutal, with soldiers goading on the Indians as if they were cattle. The sick and the old people fell by the wayside, too tired to go on. Their families were not even given time to bury them. So many thousands died along the way that to this day the Cherokee call their journey the "Trail of Tears."

Some Indians refused to go. A small group of Cherokee hid out in caves in North Carolina, and were finally allowed to stay there on a reservation. Their descendants remain in the Smoky Mountains today.

Some of the Seminole resisted, too. They had come into special disfavor with the Americans because they made a practice of sheltering slaves who ran away from southern

Sequoyah

plantations. When it came time in the 1830s for the Seminole to leave for Oklahoma, most of them went. But not all. Under a strong leader named Osceola, several hundred hid out in the Florida Everglades and carried on a hit-and-run guerrilla war that humiliated and panicked the whites.

Even though Osceola was captured by trickery in 1837 and died in prison the following year, the war went on. Many Seminole were seized and sent to Oklahoma. But a determined handful stayed on until the government finally gave up trying to pry them out. The Second Seminole War, begun in 1835, did not officially come to an end until 1934. Indians proudly call it the longest war in American history.

4
FOREST DWELLERS
The Woodlands

Nakuti was cold. The small shelter he had built for himself was warmed only by a low fire. Though it was spring, a chill wind rustled through the trees outside. Nakuti was lonely. He had spent four days and four nights alone in his tent, which stood two hours' walk from his family's camp on the shore of Lake Michigan. Most of all, Nakuti was hungry. Since he had come into the deserted woods, he had fasted, eating and drinking nothing. Sometimes he put a few pebbles under his tongue to make his mouth water, so that it would not be so dry.

Nakuti had blackened his face with ashes. This was the custom, like everything else he had done—building the small shelter, being alone, and fasting. Ever since he was five years old, he had practiced going without food, sometimes giving up one of his daily meals for several days in a row. But the earlier fasts were only preparation to harden his body and toughen his mind. This was the real thing, and his whole future depended on it.

Nakuti, now fifteen, was seeking a vision, a vision in which a supernatural being would appear to him. He hoped fervently that this Manitou, or spirit, would offer him friendly aid. If the spirit came from the sun or the morning star or a "good" animal like the bear, he would be lucky. The spirit might appear in the shape of a man, but Nakuti would know from its actions what kind of magic it was bringing him. Its power would help him the rest of his life.

Every day Nakuti's parents came to his tent to ask him whether his prayers had been answered. When they had come this morning and he had had no vision to report, he knew that they were as disappointed as he was. They were careful not to show it, though.

Nakuti was not expected to be superhuman. If no spirit had appeared to him after eight days, he would have to give up and return to his family. He could try again later, and if no vision appeared after three or four attempts, Nakuti would admit that he was not to be favored. It was not a terrible disgrace, but it meant that he would never achieve any special rank among his people.

Nakuti desperately wanted a vision. But he knew that even if one came, it might bring him bad fortune instead of good. He dreaded seeing Misikinubick, the horned serpent, for this evil Manitou bestowed the powers of sorcery. If a young man refused to accept such an evil gift, the horned serpent might reappear many times until he had his way. Nakuti's grandfather had told him a story about a youth named Teko, who had dreamed of the horned snake and had been forced to accept the gift of sorcery. Teko was told that he had to wait until he was forty years old before the magic would be his. When that time came, he had to pay for his powers by drowning his two daughters as a sacrifice. From that time on, he was much feared, since he could cripple or destroy anyone he chose to.

There were other dangers, too. Nakuti had been warned against asking for too much from a vision. According to legend, one youth had demanded that he dream about all the leaves on all the trees in the world. He asked this so that absolutely nothing would be hidden from him.

This was thought to be greedy. Though the boy got his wish, he was told that "as soon as the leaves start to fall, you will get sick. When all the leaves drop to the ground, that is the end of your life." It happened just as foretold.

And everyone knew the story of the boy who had had a vision after four days but was urged by his father to fast just one more day so that he might gain still more power. When his father appeared at his tent the next day, the youth told him that he had indeed been visited again. But the boy had been told that, because he wanted too much, he would never again appear in human form. When his father grieved, the boy went on: "I have dreamed of a robin who would have done well by me, but you forced him too far. I must leave you forever, but I will give you this comfort. I shall turn into a robin and every spring I shall perch in the tops of the pines before your lodge and sing."

Nakuti drifted off to sleep. Then, as he said later, the spirits "took pity on him" and sent him a message. A strange-looking man appeared, thickset and muscular. He had a big beaked nose. Nakuti knew him for a thunderbird, a helpful spirit who would bring him good fortune. The spirit taught Nakuti some special songs and rituals. He told him what objects he should collect for his sacred "medicine bundle"—arrows, a dried beaver skin, and certain stones. And he promised to help the youth when he was in need.

Nakuti awoke with a wonderful sense of relief and happiness. He put out his fire, packed up his few possessions and started the walk back to camp. His ordeal was over. He had been rewarded, and everyone would rejoice when he told them what had happened.

Nakuti was a Menomini (*muh*-NAHM-*uh-nee*) Indian. His people lived in what is now northern Wisconsin, near the upper end of Lake Michigan. For them and for other nearby groups—as indeed for almost all North American Indians—a person's visions and dreams were among the most important things that could ever happen.

The Menomini belonged to a widespread culture group, the Woodland Indians. The home of this group extended across the northeastern United States from the Atlantic coast to the Great Lakes, and well into Canada. Most Woodland Indians had several things in common. They hunted the game that abounded in the forests, and also did some farming. Their tribal organization was fairly simple. And they shared many similar religious beliefs.

Probably the most famous Woodland people were the Iroquois of New York State, Indians so independent and proud that they insisted on a separate declaration of war against the Germans in World War I. (Since they have never yet made peace, a second declaration for World War II was considered unnecessary.) Other Woodland peoples included the Naskapi, Montagnais, Beothuk, Micmac, and Abnaki of eastern Canada; the Pequot, Massachuset, Narraganset, and Wampanoag of New England; and the nearby Huron and Lenape (Delaware). Around the Great Lakes lived the Shawnee, Miami, Potawatomi, Fox, Winnebago, Menomini, Chippewa (Ojibway), and Cree.

A great number of Woodland Indians, from the Massachuset of the east to the Chippewa of the west, spoke languages of the Algonkian language family. This did not mean that all of these people could understand each other. But the grammar and some words were similar, indicating that the languages may have had a common ancestor. (Not all the Woodland Indians spoke an Algonkian language. The Iroquois spoke a different language, related to those of the Huron and the Cherokee.)

Because the first Indians encountered by early English settlers in North America spoke Algonkian languages, many Algonkian words have entered our language. These words tell us a lot about the way Woodland people lived.

Hominy, squash, and *succotash* are Algonkian words, just as they were Algonkian foods. So is the "pone" of *corn pone.* Women of the Woodland tribes tended small gardens, where they raised corn, beans, and squash. It was Indian farmers of New England who told the early English settlers about corn. They also showed the English how to fertilize the soil by dropping in a fish along with the corn kernels as they were planting. Indian women also gathered wild seeds,

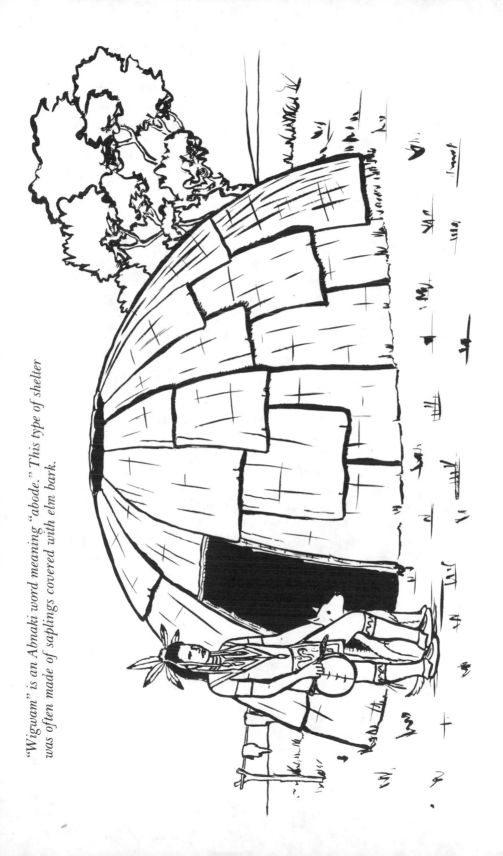

"Wigwam" is an Abnaki word meaning "abode." This type of shelter was often made of saplings covered with elm bark.

nuts, and berries. And around the small bays and inlets of Lake Superior, Indians gathered and stored quantities of wild rice. *Menomini,* in fact, means "wild rice people."

Hunting was also important to the Woodland way of life. For, even though these people grew crops, they relied heavily on game animals for their food. Throughout much of the Woodland area, deer, bear, elk, and beaver were abundant. Several animals native to North America have Algonkian names. Among them are *raccoon* (from a word meaning "hand scratcher") and *opossum* (meaning "white animal").

Along the Atlantic coast and around inland lakes and streams, fishing added to the Woodland Indians' food supply. Men often wove fish traps from reeds and branches. An early explorer of Minnesota described the Chippewa fishing this way: "From Morning till night, imagining themselves, if we may judge from appearances, the happiest mortals in existence."

Because the Woodland area was rich in natural resources, people lived well. Many of the women had time to decorate their family's buckskin clothing and containers with beautiful designs of dyed porcupine quills.

Wigwam is another Algonkian word, and was a basic form of Woodland shelter. It was made of poles covered with mats made from bark or woven reeds. The shape and material varied from tribe to tribe. Along the Atlantic coast many Indians built a dome-shaped wigwam covered with bark. Around the Great Lakes and in Canada wigwams were more often cone-shaped, and were covered with birchbark.

Birchbark was a very handy material for Woodland Indians who lived in the northern area where birches grow. They used it to make canoes, covering wooden frames with thin sheets of the light but sturdy bark. Birchbark canoes were easily carried overland between rivers or past rapids through which it was too dangerous to travel. (Farther south, Woodland Indians made dugout canoes by hollowing out logs with fire.) Woodland Indian women bent birchbark into all sorts of containers, both for storing and for cooking food. They cooked food in birchbark by dropping in hot

Making a birchbark canoe required a great deal of skill. The woman here has punched holes with a bone awl and is stitching pieces of bark together with tamarack roots. Later she will caulk the seams with tree gum to keep the boat from leaking.

stones until the contents simmered. In the spring, birchbark buckets were hung on maple trees to catch the sap that flowed, a technique white settlers were happy to learn from the Indians.

Another Algonkian word is *tomahawk,* which we usually picture as a hatchet with a scalp or two attached. In the beginning, a tomahawk was a curved wooden club with a round head, which looked somewhat like a human arm gripping a ball. It was a useful weapon for hand-to-hand combat. The Woodland tribes, like those of the Southeast, did not shy away from a fight. In time, the head of the tomahawk was made from stone. Then, after the coming of the whites, it became metal, and the hatchet shape emerged. By this time, guns had come to America, too. So the tomahawk ceased to be a weapon and turned into a symbol. It was solemnly handed about and exchanged at treaty signings and other important occasions.

Another object of importance in Woodland ceremonials was the *calumet* (CAL-*yuh-met*). This is a French word, reminding us that the French were the first Europeans to penetrate many Woodland regions. Like the tomahawk, the calumet changed over the years. Originally it was a hollow reed. An Indian smoked tobacco through it by holding it on top of a bowl of burning tobacco, which rested on the ground. A single calumet was handed around from one smoker to another. Later, the reed stem was attached to its own smoking bowl, and the calumet became what we would call a pipe.

Calumet bowls were most commonly made from a red stone called catlinite, named by the whites after a famous painter of Indians, George Catlin. Catlinite is found only in Minnesota. The quarry was a sacred place, and an Indian traveling to or from it was regarded as a sort of pilgrim on a holy mission, not to be harmed. Today the catlinite quarry is a United States national monument, and only Indians are allowed to dig out the stone.

Indian men smoked the calumet on important occasions, such as tribal gatherings or religious celebrations. Because it was smoked to symbolize friendship and agree-

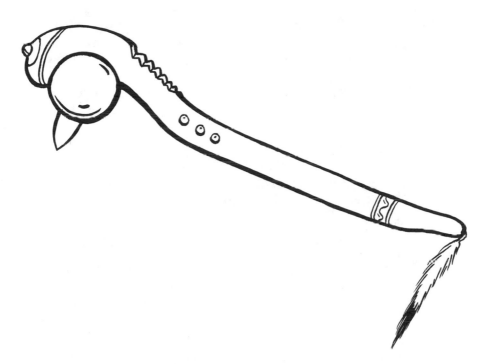

An Indian tomahawk was an efficient weapon. Sacred decorations gave it special power from the spirit world, and notches indicated its owner's exploits.

The calumet was more than a pipe. A handsome example like this one would have been kept in its own special leather pouch.

ment, it is often called a "peace pipe." Indians had other kinds of pipes, too, for more ordinary occasions. But they rarely smoked as casually as we do today. Generally a pipe was carefully removed from its safe place after a meal, especially to welcome a guest. After its owner lit it, he pointed it symbolically toward the four points of the compass. Then, if there was more than one smoker, the pipe was passed formally from one to another.

Of all Woodland ceremonial objects, perhaps the one best known to us is *wampum*—yet another Algonkian word. Wampum consists of small cylindrical beads made by drilling holes in clam shells. (The complete Indian word, *wampumpeak,* means "string of white shell beads.") Actually, a clam shell, though mainly white, is partly purple, and purple beads were always regarded as more valuable than white.

Wampum was originally used only as jewelry by New England chiefs. When the whites came, they quickly recognized its value among the Indians and began manufacturing large amounts of it, using metal drills. The Dutch were especially involved in this business. Soon the beads became a kind of money throughout the Northeast. Whites used them too, since coins were scarce in colonial America. Wampum belts—wide bands of wampum with simple designs made by combining white and purple shells—were also used to confirm alliances and as condolence gifts upon the death of a leader. If you visit the Museum of the American Indian in New York City, you can see wampum belts that the Lenape Indians exchanged with William Penn in 1682, when they transferred thousands of acres of Pennsylvania land to the whites. Wampum was manufactured well into the 1800s at the Campbell factory in Pascack (now Park Ridge), New Jersey.

The Algonkian word *Manitou* is usually translated as "Great Spirit." White missionaries tended to think of "Manitou" as "God," but the two were not the same. Some people explain Manitou (which the Iroquois called *orenda)* as an impersonal power in the universe, a sort of spiritual electricity. We think of harnessing a force like this to do what we want it to do. But the Indian idea was to "get in touch with"

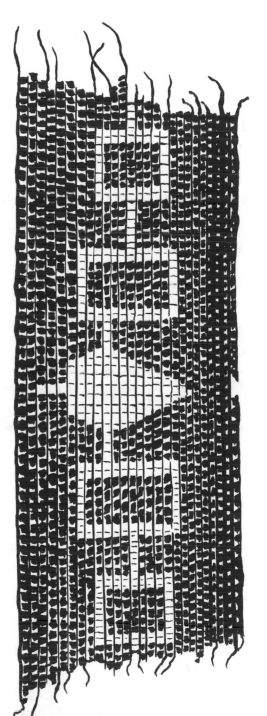

Among some Indians, wampum belts were used to record tribal legends and history. This belt would have been regarded as quite valuable because the purple shells far outnumber the white ones.

Manitou and thus be at one with the driving spirit of the universe. It would probably be more "Indian" to think of many Manitous—to think of supernatural power in terms of individual occasions and beings. Thus steam could be a Manitou, and so could an arrow that goes straight to the mark, or a flame caught in an updraft, or a warrior victorious in battle.

The only true test of Manitou in operation was whether it worked. If an Indian succeeded, Manitou had helped. If an Indian failed, Manitou had abandoned him or her. The Indians were generally willing to put a new Manitou to the test, as this story shows: In the 1660s a French missionary traveled into the country of the Fox Indians in Wisconsin. He told them that Jesus Christ, as symbolized by the cross, was a powerful Manitou. The Indians eagerly adopted the cross, painting it on their bodies when they went out to fight the Sioux. They won a victory over their enemies, and returned praising the Jesus Manitou. But the following year, painted as before, the Fox braves suffered a stinging defeat at the hands of the Sioux. So the Fox rejected the white people's Manitou. They tore down the cross that the missionary had put up in their village and refused to let the priest back in.

A vision quest, like that of Nakuti described at the beginning of this chapter, was a very common way of experiencing Manitou. Among tribes around the Great Lakes, adolescents were expected to undergo at least one such vigil. Girls did so when they first menstruated, hoping for a spirit that would predict marriage to a powerful man or the birth of strong and healthy children. Among tribes in other areas, only mature men sought visions. Nakuti was expected to describe his dream. Most Indians, however, kept this experience to themselves. The Yuma Indians said that "if a man tells his dream, it passes with the day"—that is, the Manitou disappears with the telling. Sometimes a single vision lasted a lifetime. More often, Indians sought this kind of experience at many crucial periods in their lives.

Among most Southwest tribes, priests were an important link with the world of spirits. In the Southeast, both priests and shamans, each group in a different way, helped ordinary people deal with or acquire spiritual power. Few Woodland tribes had priests at all. But shamans were all-important, especially for curing the sick. Some Woodland Indians maintained organizations somewhat like the kachina societies of the Southwest. The Midewiwin (*mih*-DAY-*wih-win*), or "Grand Medicine Societies," of the Chippewa were open to both men and women who wanted to become experts at healing disease. There were four steps, or degrees. A member could begin each step only with a payment to the healer in charge of the medicine society. At each step, a member had to memorize a great many prayers and other rituals that were supposed to cure illness. These took so long to learn, and the payments were so high, that few Indians ever reached the fourth and final step.

Each year, in the spring or fall, there were public displays at which members could show off their skills. One old man described such a ceremony he had attended as a youth. His father, an important man in the Midewiwin, rose from his place and walked around his tent. After he sat down, a big round stone moved, rolling over and over as it followed the trail of his father. To us, of course, a rolling white stone has little to do with curing illness, but apparently such displays had a powerful psychological effect on people who saw them. "I saw it happen several times," recalled the old man, "and others saw it also."

Another healing organization was the False Face Society of the Iroquois. Its members, both men and women, danced and chanted to drive away illness. They wore masks representing mythological forest beings who had the power to cure disease. The beings had curious distorted features, with popping eyes and crooked mouths. Like the kachinas, specific characters were represented in traditional ways—among them Crooked Face, Spoon Mouth, and Wind. The most powerful masks were those in which carving was begun on the trunk of a living tree.

The Algonkian word *sachem* (SAY-*chum*) meant a kind of chief, who inherited his position. Among most Woodland tribes, chiefs were not terribly powerful. Tribal organization

This Iroquois False Face mask, decorated with human hair, is a representation of a grotesque forest creature.

was weaker and simpler than in the Southeast. To regard sachems as kings, which the English did, is not really accurate. They were respected elders, often known as "grandfathers," who gave advice in a *powwow*. (This Algonkian word had several meanings; it is used here in one of the commonest—a political council or conference.) This is not to say that a strong sachem could not rule his people. But he could not do it merely by being a sachem. He had to prove himself in battle, to demonstrate that he had the aid of Manitou. He had to show that he had power, not simply by being the son of his father, but by earning it himself.

There is one great exception to weak tribal organization among the Woodland tribes, and that is the Iroquois. Though originally they may have lived much as other Woodland tribes, around the middle 1500s they developed the famous Iroquois League. For a long time this was the most powerful Indian organization north of the Rio Grande.

The Iroquois dominated the region around Lake Ontario. Their Algonkian enemies in the area gave them the name by which we know them; it means "real snakes." But they called themselves *Hodenosaunee*, meaning "people of the long house." This term referred partly to their dwellings. They lived not in wigwams, but in long bark-covered structures that sheltered many families. The term referred also to the League itself. Like the Iroquois house, it united into one community individuals that still maintained their independence.

The Iroquois tribes were, from east to west, the Mohawk, known as "Keepers of the Eastern Door"; the Oneida, "Second to Join the League"; the Onondaga, "Those Who Watch Over the Central Fire"; the Cayuga, "Younger Brothers of the League"; and the Seneca, "Keepers of the Western Door." Together they were known as the Five Nations. When they were joined in the early 1700s by the Tuscarora of North Carolina ("Those Who Came Later from the South"), they became the Six Nations.

According to Iroquois tradition, the League was formed by two men, Deganawidah and Hiawatha, in the late 1500s. Deganawidah was a Huron who had a vision of peace and

An Iroquois long house might be 100 feet in length. Inside, each family had its own separate compartment.

brotherhood, to be achieved through justice and fair dealing among peoples. When he was born, his mother was told that he would indirectly cause the ruin of her people. She tried three times to drown him, without success. Since Deganawidah was an outcast among the Huron, he began traveling among other peoples. Somewhere he met Hiawatha, who was apparently a real person and a Mohawk (not the Chippewa hero described in the poem by Longfellow). Deganawidah had a speech impediment, while Hiawatha's wonderful oratory could win over the most hostile audiences.

Deganawidah and Hiawatha together persuaded five Indian groups, or nations, to join in a league of friendship, renouncing warfare and bloodshed among themselves. According to one legend, the Onondaga were among the hardest to persuade. In order to convince them, Deganawidah is said to have put out the sun and darkened the sky. This miraculous event may have been an eclipse.

However the League was actually formed, we know that its council consisted of fifty sachems, with a specified number from each of the member nations. They assembled always in Onondaga territory. They met whenever necessary but at least every five years. The sachems were chosen from each nation by the elder women, for Iroquois women had a good deal of power. When the sachems met, the Mohawk opened the discussion, and then all the sachems talked things over. Decisions were always unanimous. If at first there was disagreement, discussion simply continued until everyone agreed upon a course of action.

The Iroquois had a reputation for fierceness and cruelty. They did make a practice of torturing prisoners, like the southeasterners. Great Lakes tribes such as the Chippewa despised the Iroquois because of this custom. But even the whites had to admit, as one Frenchman put it, that they were "the fiercest and most formidable people in North America, and at the same time as shrewd as could be imagined."

In that part of the Woodland Indian region first settled

by whites—the Atlantic coast from the Carolinas northward
to the St. Lawrence River—there were probably no more
than 125,000 Indians. A plague had killed thousands of
them in Massachusetts not long before the coming of white
settlers.

Nevertheless, initially it would have been easy for the
Indians to wipe out the tiny settlements in Virginia and New
England as the English pioneers struggled against hunger
and disease. And it would have been equally simple to
destroy the French newcomers in Canada before their small
outposts had taken hold.

Instead, the Indians extended the hand of friendship.
Not long after the Pilgrims arrived, an Indian named
Samoset wandered into Plymouth and astonished them by
calling out "Welcome, Englishmen." (He had learned the
words from a trader.) In a few days he returned to introduce
the local Wampanoag sachem, Massasoit, and a group of
braves. Among them was Squanto, who had spent time in
London after an English sea captain had carried him off into
slavery.

In the south, the Jamestown settlers were welcomed by
Powhatan, whose people controlled much of Virginia. There
is a legend that his daughter Pocahontas saved the life of
John Smith when her father threatened to have him killed.
But Smith was a great storyteller, so it's not certain what
actually happened. Relations between whites and Indians in
Virginia were friendly at first. Pocahontas herself married a
colonist, John Rolfe, and went to England, where she soon
died. Her son, through his only daughter, founded the
Randolph family, one of the most prestigious families of
Virginia.

It did not take long for the Indians to realize that their
future was in danger. White settlers were coming in ever
greater numbers. They were taking Indian land and destroying the wild game on which Indian life depended. They
brought with them new and strange diseases (measles, for
instance) that destroyed whole bands of Indians.

Armed resistance to the whites began in Virginia. After
Powhatan died, his son Opechancanough determined to

drive the English out. He attacked in the 1620s and again in the 1640s. But he was decisively beaten the second time. In New England the Pequot of the Connecticut River Valley attacked the whites in 1637. The Pequot War—actually, just a few skirmishes—ended quickly, with the colonists victorious. In both these uprisings, the whites had the aid of other Indians, who were eager to ally themselves with the powerful newcomers in order to get revenge on their Indian enemies.

This was what happened to "King" Philip, the son of the sachem Massasoit. In the case of the Wampanoag, as with other New England tribes, Indian-white relations had become bitter. When the settlers no longer depended on the Indians for food and other help, they tried to force them to adopt English customs, laws, and religion. At Plymouth, for example, Indians were forbidden to hunt, fish, or carry burdens on the Sabbath.

Philip's brother had become sachem after their father's death, but he himself died soon afterward. Philip thought the whites had poisoned his brother. He convinced several bands to join him and went to war in 1675. For months the conflict raged, with Indians swooping down for sudden raids on colonial towns and whites fighting back. In Rhode Island, the colonists, led by an Indian who agreed to betray his people, attacked and burned a Narraganset village. According to a colonial writer, more than 600 Indians were "terribly Barbikew'd."

Indians did not like to carry on long wars. As time went on, Philip's allies melted away, many to hunt, fish, and plant gardens because their provisions were running out. Other bands, captured by the whites, agreed to fight alongside the colonists. And so, in 1676, the colonists were able to surround Philip himself and shoot him. They cut off his head and carried it proudly to Plymouth. There, mounted on a pole, it remained on display for twenty-five years.

It is easy to see why there were few Indians left along the Atlantic coast by 1700. War and disease wiped out many. Typhoid fever killed a third of the Micmac, for example. Many Indians intermarried with whites and lost their identity. Still others moved westward. Only in the more remote areas of Canada were Woodland groups able to escape the worst results of white contact. And even there, old ways changed. Peoples like the Cree became totally dependent on trading furs to the whites for their livelihood.

The Iroquois, as usual, played a special role. In the early 1600s they came in contact with the Dutch, who started trading guns with them in exchange for furs. The League was then only a few decades old, but it soon flowered and the Iroquois became the most powerful Indians in the Northeast. Since the Iroquois themselves had few furs, they quickly took over weaker tribes that were good at fur trapping. If force was necessary, it was used, and in this way the Iroquois almost wiped out the Huron in the 1640s.

For almost 150 years, the Iroquois—wealthy, proud, and strong—played a key role in colonial America. Their location in northern New York was a strategic one, between the French in Canada and the English in what is now the United States. When France and England went to war late in the 1600s, their conflicts in Europe and Asia were reflected in the New World. The series of four wars in America, from 1689 to 1763, are known as the French and Indian Wars because of the role the Indians played.

For a long time the Iroquois had been at odds with their Algonkian-speaking neighbors. So when the Algonkians allied themselves with the French, the Iroquois sided with the English. Although they cleverly refrained from doing much actual fighting, the fact that the Iroquois did not aid the French was of great value to the English. And the Iroquois did actually take up arms in the last French and Indian War.

Like the Creek, the Iroquois benefited from their alliance with the English for a few years. But, also like the Creek, their final period of glory did not last long. They were divided during the American Revolution, the Oneida and Tuscarora favoring the Americans and the other four "nations" siding with the English. When the English were defeated, most of the Iroquois moved to Canada. But their great days were over.

Events in the east soon affected Indians in the Great Lakes area. At first there were only indirect ripples as displaced Indians from the coast moved into the forests and prairies west of the Appalachians. Grudgingly, the Indians farther west made room for refugee Lenape and Huron.

In the Ohio Valley, Algonkian peoples such as the Ottawa, Chippewa, and Potawatomi had long been friendly with the French. Since these Europeans came for trade but not for land, whites and Indians lived fairly peacefully side by side for many years. It was these Indians who aided the French against the English during the French and Indian Wars. Trouble came as the French faced defeat in the last of these wars.

During the conflict, which lasted from 1754 to 1763, the English drove the French out of their Ohio Valley forts, including Detroit. The French had been generous with trade goods—guns, ammunition, and rum—whereas the English were stingy. English policy was strongly opposed to "purchasing the good behavior of the Indians by presents." Pontiac, an Ottawa Indian and a spellbinding orator, traveled from tribe to tribe stirring them up against the English. One of the ways he roused his audiences was to describe the vision of a Delaware shaman. This man, said Pontiac, dreamed that Manitou was unhappy that the English were living in the Indians' land, and urged the Indians to "send them back to the lands which I have created for them."

Pontiac attacked the English in May of 1763. In a few short weeks his warriors seized all the British forts except two. These—Detroit and Fort Pitt (Pittsburgh)—they besieged. The British commander, Lord Jeffrey Amherst, hastily sent reinforcements west. He was so enraged that he considered infecting the Indians with smallpox "by means of blankets." He would have set dogs upon them except that England was "at too great a distance to think of that at present." (Apparently manhunting dogs were not available in the colonies.)

As the summer wore on, Pontiac's fighting force grew smaller. He and his main army were concentrated at Detroit, but the Indians had no patience for a long siege. Many bands deserted. A final blow was the news that the French had finally lost the war and signed a peace treaty with the British. Pontiac had hoped all along that his former allies would return to the Ohio Valley. He surrendered in the fall, and was allowed to live out his short life among his people.

Woodland Indian resistance to the whites was not completely broken, however. Settlers flooded into the Ohio Valley in the late 1700s, and several conflicts broke out. Among the Indian leaders was the Miami chief, Little Turtle. He and his warriors dealt hard blows to the whites in the early 1790s. But their defeat at the decisive Battle of Fallen Timbers in 1795 forced them to give up their Ohio lands. At the treaty signing, Little Turtle, reminded of his long struggle against the intruders, replied: "I am the last to sign the treaty. I will be the last to break it."

One Indian who witnessed his people's humiliation in Ohio was Tecumseh of the Shawnee. A man of immense pride and intelligence, he was determined to resist the whites. Tecumseh had the sense to realize that no one tribe, or even small groups of tribes, could drive out the whites. *All* the Indians had to unite and think of themselves first as Indians and only second as Shawnee or Miami or Winnebago. He once said to the whites after Indians had signed a treaty he believed to be a fraud:

> The Being within, communing with past ages, tells me that once there were no white men on this continent. Then it all belonged to the red men, children of the same parents. They were placed on it by the Great Spirit, who made them to keep it, to cross it, to enjoy it, and to fill it with the same race. It was once a happy race, but has been made miserable by the white people, who are never contented, but always taking over.
>
> The way, and the only way, to check and to stop this evil is for all red men to unite in claiming a common and equal right in the land, as it was at first and should be yet. It was never divided, but belongs to all for the use of each. The white people have no right to take the land from the Indians, because the Indians had it first and it is theirs.[1]

Tecumseh

Tecumseh had a brother, the Prophet, a shaman inspired by frequent visions of the spirit world. The two men traveled about the Middle West and South for years trying to unite the Indians against the whites. Many Indians responded. You have read about what happened to the Creek. Their northern brothers fared no better. In 1811, when Tecumseh was traveling in the South, the governor of Indiana, William Henry Harrison, defeated the Prophet at the Battle of Tippecanoe in northern Indiana.

Tecumseh, swearing "the eternal hatred of an avenger," continued to organize, and won many Indians to the British side against the Americans in the War of 1812. He commanded a dedicated band of followers, often more eager for combat than the British themselves. But Tecumseh, like Philip and Pontiac before him, was doomed. In a battle between the British and Americans in southern Canada, Tecumseh met his death. He was first heard yelling "like a tiger" and urging his braves to attack. Then he was seen badly wounded, and then was seen no more. His body was never found, and there were rumors that he lived on. But his dream of Indian unity was dead.

Most of the Woodland Indians who survived were very poor, without leadership and without hope. Small bands were given reservations in the United States and Canada. Many were moved west of the Mississippi into the Indian territory of Oklahoma. How they fared in their new life will be described in the last chapter.

5

HUNTERS IN A FROZEN LAND

The Subarctic

In the silence of the empty plain, nothing could be heard but the rhythmic swoosh of snowshoes and the howling of a far-off wolf pack. It was only two hours past noon. But the light was fading fast and soon it would be dark. The small band of eighteen men, women, and children was heading westward over the snow, in the direction of the setting sun. Their goal was a nearby lake. Its surface would be frozen, but the men and boys would chop holes and fish through them, for the people had run out of food. They had eaten the last of their caribou meat three days ago. This morning some of them were so hungry that they had gnawed on strips of skin from their own tents.

The tents—and indeed just about all the possessions of the band—were carried by the women and girls as they trudged westward. That way the males of the group were free to use their bows and arrows on any game they might happen to see.

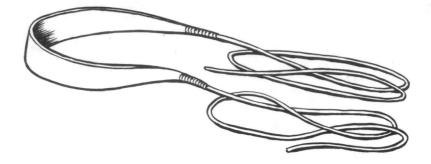

A tumpline, steadied across the forehead or shoulders, helped people carry very heavy loads. With it, almost any bundle could be turned into a sort of back pack.

White Marten was eleven, and this was the first time she had had to pull a toboggan load. Up to now she had carried just a small pack on her back, but her older sister had died a few days ago, and the group needed a strong pair of arms. The young girl grieved for her sister. She and her mother had wrapped the body in skins and her father had placed it in a tree. All of them hoped that her spirit was at peace and would not return to trouble them.

Pulling a toboggan was not easy work in the cold and snow, but White Marten felt a certain pride in being treated like a grown-up. Her mother's load was much heavier—a hundred pounds steadied by a tumpline. The strip of moose hide was stretched across her forehead and under her backpack of tent skins and household gear.

White Marten had once seen an Eskimo family with a toboggan pulled by a team of dogs. But she knew that her people were not allowed to use dogs in this way. Her father had told her why.

Long ago there was only one woman in the world, and she lived in a cave. After a while, a doglike creature came into her cave. When he turned into a handsome young man, the woman fell in love with him and they had a child. But then a giant appeared out of nowhere. He killed the young man and tore him into bits. After that the giant threw the man's flesh onto the land, where it turned into animals. His internal organs, tossed into the sea, became fish. And when the giant flung the skin into the air, lo and behold, the sky was filled with birds.

The giant told the woman that her offspring could hunt and eat as many of these creatures as they needed to. This was how White Marten's people had been created, and why they could kill animals and fish and birds. But, since their world was made from a creature like a dog, they had to treat this animal with special care.

White Marten's thoughts were interrupted when, over a ridge not far away, there suddenly appeared another small band of people. The two groups knew each other because they had sometimes hunted together. But instead of going forward and meeting, the bands sat down in silence several feet apart on the frozen ground, huddling into their furs for warmth. Finally a man from the other band stood and gave an account of what had happened to them since their last meeting. One youth had drowned in an icy stream. An old woman, too sick to travel, had to be left behind to die alone. No caribou could be found, and famine seemed about to kill them all.

Next White Marten's father stood to tell about their own bad luck. He described how White Marten's older sister had died, and how they too had run out of food. The stories were greeted with mournful wails.

Again there was silence, but only a short one, as if people were saying a brief amen. Then the two bands walked quickly toward each other and exchanged hearty greetings. With the bad news out of the way, they could concentrate on gossip, games, and tall tales. Some branches and twigs were found, a fire was started, and a bit of tobacco was exchanged. The night passed in friendly companionship. Hunger could be forgotten for the time being.

White Marten's people were the Chipewyan of northern Canada. They probably had the most extensive territory of any Indian tribe in America—over 2,500 square miles, just west of Hudson Bay. They belonged to a culture group called the Subarctic ("below the Arctic"). These people occupied most of central and western Canada, as well as large parts of Alaska. The main groups in this vast region, along with the Chipewyan, included the Slave, Yellowknife, Beaver, Dogrib, Hare, Kutchin, and Tanana. All these Indians spoke languages of the Athabascan family—as do the Navajo and Apache of the Southwest.

The land of the Subarctic Indians is a harsh one. In the north lies the tundra, where no trees grow at all. In the south is the taiga, a country of low spruces and other hardy plants, where a tree can grow for 200 years and still be no taller than a man's head. The region well deserves its Indian name, which means the Barren Grounds.

Winters in the Subarctic, which last over eight months, bring high winds, snow, and temperatures as low as 80 degrees below zero Fahrenheit. A December day may have less than six hours of light. The brief summers are hot, with temperatures reaching 90 degrees and clouds of fierce mosquitoes. In June or July the days are twenty hours long. Over the ground—permanently frozen below a depth of about fifteen inches—roam moose, caribou, bear, wolves, and musk-oxen. The region is also the home of rabbits, hares, martens, snowy owls, and ptarmigan.

Since hardly anything edible grows in the Subarctic, the Indians who lived there were almost totally dependent on hunting and fishing for their food. Game animals were the best source for a nourishing diet. But, as a Chipewyan proverb put it, "No man knows the way of the wind and the caribou." So the people had to move constantly in search of prey. Because these Indians relied so heavily on hunting and moved around so much, their culture resembled closely that of the very first people who crossed the land bridge from Asia to America.

Many Subarctic peoples, such as White Marten's band, relied very heavily on caribou. These large animals of the deer family moved in herds onto the tundra in late summer and early fall. This was when the Indians would concentrate their hunts. In the winter, when the caribou moved into the forest, the Subarctic people usually relied on fish for survival. In the west, near the Pacific coast, Subarctic Indians had a surer supply of rich salmon, so they depended less on hunting.

When hunting caribou, small bands of Indians would combine to form larger groups. Men would drive stakes into the ground to make a sort of funnel-shaped corral, with a large end about three miles across. Then they would goad the animals forward into this trap until they were penned into a narrow space where they could be slaughtered. The number of caribou killed was truly enormous. Even in modern times, Dogrib hunters near Great Slave Lake killed over 50,000 caribou in a ten-year period. This averaged out to over 37 caribou per hunter per year.

Indians killed large animals like caribou, moose, and bear with bows and arrows. For smaller game, they made traps or used snares constructed of *babiche* (*buh*-BEESH). This French term originated with the courageous fur trappers, who were the first Europeans to penetrate much of northern Canada. It describes a kind of thong that Indian women cut out of caribou hide.

Another use for babiche was in making snowshoes, which were as necessary to Subarctic peoples as cars are to

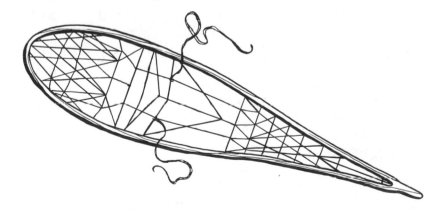

Snowshoes enabled Indians to walk on top of deep drifts without sinking in. Among Subarctic peoples, a snowshoe might be as long as four feet, and over a foot wide.

us. The gracefully curved frames, made of birch, were laced with babiche. Winter travel also depended on toboggans. Indians made these flat sleds from thin slabs of birch or juniper. If wood was lacking, they made do with frozen animal skins. In the summer, people traveled on the many lakes and rivers of the Subarctic in slim birchbark canoes. These canoes were so light that a man could carry one slung across his shoulders.

Naturally enough, the Subarctic Indians had little use for elaborate houses. Most of the year they lived in a sort of rounded tipi made of animal skins lashed together with babiche. Since trees weren't very plentiful, they carried the bent poles along with them when they traveled. A woman could set up the frame and cover it in just a few minutes. She might pack this shelter on the outside with snow for extra warmth. A fire was kindled in the center, and smoke escaped out of an opening left at the top. Actually, in frigid weather, the fire often caused a downdraft of cold air, and some people found it warmer to sleep outside—well wrapped in fur robes.

The clothes worn by Subarctic Indians had some interesting features. For one thing, they were tailored—trousers were cut to fit the leg, and upper garments were shaped to fit the arms and torso. No other Indians wore tailored clothing, and in fact, neither did Europeans until the Middle Ages. Apparently the art of tailoring originated in Asia and then moved westward into Europe and eastward in America. The Eskimo made tailored clothes, and taught the Subarctic Indians how to do so.

Subarctic clothing was warm and practical. For instance, mittens were attached to a kind of shoulder harness so that they wouldn't get lost. We have this arrangement for absentminded children, but to the Indians it could be a matter of life and death, especially in a blinding blizzard. Another good feature (still used in children's sleepwear) was joining the feet to the legs—in this case, moccasins to leggings. Over this two-in-one garment men wore a shirt or parka. The name *Chipewyan* is from a Cree word meaning "pointed skins," because a man's upper garment dangled to

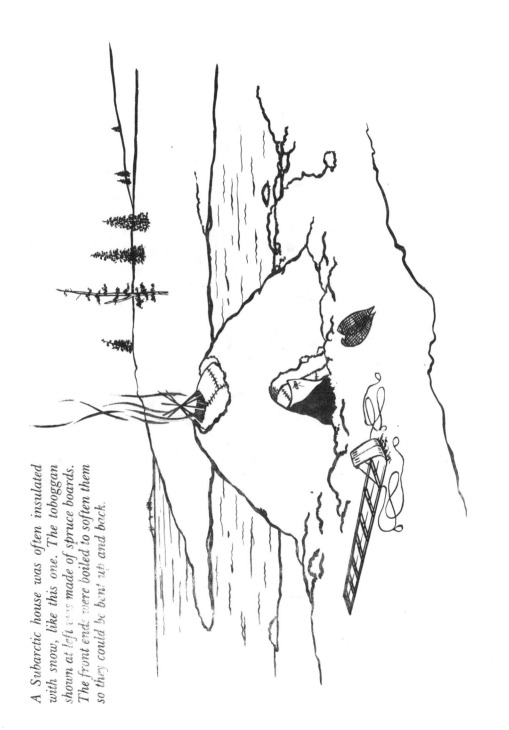

A Subarctic house was often insulated with snow, like this one. The toboggan shown at left was made of spruce boards. The front ends were boiled to soften them so they could be bent up and back.

The shirt of a Subarctic hunter dipped to a distinctive point. This man is well equipped with musket and powder horn. The sheath that holds his knife is beautifully decorated with porcupine quills.

a point front and back. (Other Subarctic tribes wore similar shirts.) Women wore a longish dress over their leggings. All these garments were made of caribou skin, or sometimes moose hide. To be well clothed and well equipped in the Subarctic, a person needed about twenty caribou skins a year. Extra warmth was added with robes, ponchos, and turbans made of fur.

Because of their nomadic, hand-to-mouth existence, the Subarctic Indians had to cook and eat simply. Sometimes they roasted meat by holding it on sticks over the fire. More often, they boiled it, melting snow for water. The commonest method was to dig a hole in the ground and line it with a caribou stomach. Then hot stones were dropped in until the water boiled. The same technique was used with birchbark containers. Cooking this way was slow. Besides, white travelers complained, the food was apt to be a bit gritty from the stones. It is no wonder that metal cooking pots later became a popular trade item.

One thing White Marten's band must have kept their eyes out for on their wanderings was a *cache* (CASH). This was the French term for a store of dried or frozen food wrapped in a skin bag and hung from a pole or tree to keep it out of the reach of animals. If a band had extra food, or simply too much to carry, the surplus might be stored in this way. Although it was considered the property of whoever stored it, any people in need were permitted to help themselves.

Subarctic Indians did not have the time or the energy for elaborate crafts and complex religious ceremonies. They had no political organization, though a leader might be chosen for a big hunting expedition or a war party. (They frequently fought with the Eskimo.)

For the Subarctic peoples, as with most Indians, marriage was strictly a matter of economics. Survival depended on the tasks a husband and wife performed for each other and their children. Men did the hunting and fishing. Women did just about everything else. One of the first Europeans to travel in the land of the Chipewyan was Samuel Hearne, an Englishman who worked for the Hudson's Bay Company. Sent out to explore the country in the 1770s, he made two unsuccessful trips with a few male companions. Then he found an Indian guide who explained the problem. Such journeys were bound to fail, said the guide, unless there were women along:

> Women were made for labor. One of them can carry or haul as much as two men can. They also pitch our tents, make and mend our clothing, and keep us warm at night. In fact, there is no such thing as traveling any considerable distance, or for any length of time, in this country without their assistance. And, though they do everything, they are maintained at little expense. For, while they stand cooking, the very licking of their fingers in scarce times is enough to keep them alive.[1]

Hearne commented that, "however odd this may appear, it is but too true a description of the situation of women in this country." He did think, though, that the cooks probably snatched a few extra bites of food when their menfolk weren't watching.

The harsh lot of women was one of the worst things about Subarctic culture. Men prized them for the work they could do, but they gambled them away as if they were animals. The Chipewyan used to stage wrestling matches, with their wives as prizes. A woman had to go with the winner no matter how she felt about it. Mothers sometimes even killed girl babies to spare them future suffering.

Being a woman was bad enough, but being old or sick was even worse. (And "old" happened early, since the average life-span among Subarctic people was thirty years.) When an individual couldn't perform the expected chores—whether hunting or hauling—or just move from one place to another, the band was in trouble. If possible, the ailing person might be pulled on a toboggan. But this couldn't be done for very long. The band eventually had to leave the old or ailing behind. Usually such a person asked to be abandoned, and the group left a supply of firewood for the last days on earth. It was a lonely way to die. But, as Hearne said, the custom was due to "necessity and self-preservation," not lack of humanity.

The Subarctic peoples did not believe in a heaven, but they did believe in reincarnation. A human being might be reborn either as another human or as an animal. A Kutchin woman of eighty described her experience when everyone thought she was dying:

> I left my body lying in the tent and I rose up into the air. Something was bothering me. I had to find a new mother, some woman who was going to have a baby. I thought of Rowena, Andrew's wife. She was a good girl and would be a good mother. But she was not going to have a baby. Nobody in camp was. I could not be born again. I had to go back. I went down through the wall of the tent, and back into my body, and I woke up here, still sick.[2]

If a Tanana hunter encountered an animal he couldn't kill, he assumed that this was because the animal had a human spirit. Even if animals didn't have this special quality, they were always treated with respect. For Subarctic Indians believed that animals *allowed* themselves to be killed. Since they were so cooperative, people had to take care not to offend them. Most groups had religious taboos against eating at least one kind of animal. For example, a Dogrib, even if starving, would eat no member of the weasel family. The Slave would never kill wolves if they could avoid it. And before a Chipewyan woman butchered a caribou, she had to pierce one of its eyeballs to prevent its spirit from reporting its fate to other caribou.

Men who went out hunting or fishing relied not only on their own skill but also on charms and omens. For instance, each fishing net was believed to have its own personality, and the nets were not joined together for fear one might be jealous of the other. Though the main task of shamans was to prevent and cure disease, they also made predictions about where game might be found. One method was to burn an arrow to charcoal, then place the ashes on a moose bone and set them on fire. If the shaman smelled burning meat, the hunt would be successful.

The Subarctic Indians were luckier than most when the whites came. Their land did not attract many settlers, so they were not forced off or put on small reserves. What did change was their way of making a living. The whites, who came early in the 1700s, wanted furs. The English came from the east and set up trading posts around Hudson Bay. The Russians came trom the west and established settlements on the Pacific coast and along rivers in the interior of Alaska. The Indians eagerly exchanged furs for metal goods of all kinds, including guns. And, as usual, they also received some devastating imports. One was alcohol. The other was disease, especially tuberculosis, smallpox, and influenza.

For the most part, though, the Indians of the Subarctic area were able to continue their traditional ways as nomadic hunters for many decades. American purchase of Alaska in 1867 made little difference in the everyday life of the Indians there. Only in the early 1900s did change come more noticeably. The last chapter describes what this meant for the Indians of this region.

6

PROUD RIDERS

The Plains

Last evening the band of Cheyenne men had arrived at a small clump of trees along the river and built a crude shelter, where they spent the night. They had covered their makeshift lodge with leafy branches so that it would blend with the surroundings and not be seen. For the Cheyenne were in enemy territory. Scouts had reported yesterday that just two hours from this spot lay a Crow encampment. It would be their target for tomorrow's dawn attack.

Now, as the shadows were lengthening in the August dusk, it was time to get ready. Eighteen of the twenty-one men were going on the raid. The others, inexperienced youths, would wait behind, guarding the raiders' horses. These would be of no use to the attackers, for horses—stolen out from under the enemy's noses—were the object of this raid. If the Cheyenne were lucky, everyone would have an ample choice of mounts to ride back here on.

Each warrior was careful in making preparations. Were his weapons in order? Bowstrings were tested, arrows sighted to be sure they were straight. (The Cheyenne, though they made good bows, had a saying that any kind of bow might serve, but that without straight arrows a warrior was helpless.) Arrows, differently marked for each man, were tucked into a shoulder quiver. A war club dangled from each belt. Last-minute sharpening readied each knife.

Since this was not a war party, and the men were not traveling on horseback, lances and buffalo-hide shields would be left behind with the three guards. So would the men's war shirts and the war bonnets that belonged to White Hawk, the leader of the raid, and Bald-Faced Bull. But other preparations were like those taken before a battle.

Each raider painted his face and body with symbols that had special meaning for him, dipping his fingers first into buffalo fat and then into bags of powdered paint. White Hawk drew lines on his cheeks to symbolize hawk wings. On his chest he painted other markings indicating war honors and his membership in the Kit Fox Society. If he had been leading a mounted war party, he and his men would have painted their horses as well.

Around White Hawk's neck hung his own personal medicine pouch. It contained sacred objects revealed to him in a dream. For, like the Indians of the Woodlands, the Cheyenne and their neighbors were seekers after visions. In fact, this raid was taking place because White Hawk had dreamt about it. (Of course, his people needed horses, so the need may have had something to do with the dream.) At any rate, his dream had inspired him to organize the raiding party. As the man in charge he was called the "pipeholder" because he carried a sacred pipe and tobacco. Before the men had left their own big encampment eight days ago, he had spent a night alone on a nearby hilltop. There he had prayed for success and cut out a small disk of flesh from his arm as a sacrifice.

The painting, medicine pouches, and prayers were not simply to bring luck. They prepared each warrior to meet death properly, if it should occur. After all, no one could be sure what might happen if the raiding party ran into trouble. Last year a barking dog had awakened a sleeping Sioux camp in the middle of a raid. The twelve Cheyenne warriors had had to fight their way out on foot. One was killed, and not a single horse was captured for all their trouble.

Darkness had fallen and it was time to go. With White Hawk leading, the men left the temporary camp in single file. They walked silently but swiftly through tall fields of grass until they came to the Crow village. Crouching at the outskirts, they saw that most of the tipis were dark. In a few the occupants were still up and about. Lit by firelight from within, the tipis formed great glowing cones in the night.

Luckily there was no moon and, as far as White Hawk could tell, no sentry. Most of the Crow ponies were grazing in a pasture to one side of the camp. But each tent had at least one horse tethered right outside. These were the animals most prized by their owners. Kicking Bear and five other Cheyenne were to seize as many horses as they could from the herd, using the extra bridles they had brought with them. The other men were to take what horses they could from the village itself.

The Cheyenne waited for the last campfire to be put out. Then they waited some more. Finally, nerves strained in anticipation, White Hawk gave the signal. The men crept out of their hiding places. In the first hint of dawn, their dark shadows scurried from tent to tent. Fifteen prize war-horses were led quickly away from the village, their whinnies quieted with soothing strokes. Kicking Bear and his detachment separated ten horses from the herd. With light beginning to show in the east, the raiders mounted horses, leading the extras behind them, and galloped off to their base. There was no time to lose. The Crow would already be discovering their loss and organizing a party to find the marauders.

Regrouping at the base camp, the entire party set off quickly. They rode all day and all night, changing horses twice, before sleeping. The farther they got from the Crow, the more releaxed they allowed themselves to be. Covers-His-Face told how he had taken the fine bay he was now riding. Its Crow owner had tied the horse's bridle to his own wrist to guard him while he slept, but Covers-His-Face had managed to cut the thong while the Crow snored away in his tipi. (Luckily tent skins were rolled up from the bottom in warm weather, and those inside could be seen, and heard, in the dimness.) Everyone laughed at Iron Bull, who, finding that he had captured a mare by mistake, wanted to return to the Crow village in broad daylight to get himself a stallion.

When the Cheyenne reached home a week later, they were ready for the feasting and dancing that greeted their return. They had added to the band's stock of horses, to its tales of successful exploits, and—most important of all—to its pride in the daring and resourcefulness of its people.

The Cheyenne—and the Crow and the Sioux—lived on the Great Plains. This dry, almost treeless area extends from the Mississippi River to the Rocky Mountains, and from southern Canada almost to the Gulf of Mexico. Plains tribes, the best known of all Indians, have become famous throughout the world as courageous horsemen and skillful hunters. To millions, the feathered war bonnet of the Plainsman is *the* symbol that means "Indian."

The Plains Indians had not always been horsemen. But they had always been hunters. Like the tribes of the Subarctic, they were nomads, but their prey was buffalo rather than caribou. The grasslands of the Plains fed millions of buffalo.

In time, however, the Plains people, like most other Indians, learned how to farm as well as hunt. Since so much of their homeland was dry, they settled in villages along the banks of the Mississippi and the Missouri rivers, and near smaller rivers that fed into these. Here there was enough moisture to water fields of corn, beans, squash, and pumpkins. Most of the year the people lived in large earth lodges. These round huts, partly underground, were built of branches and earth packed over solid wood foundation posts. In the summer, the people moved west to the High Plains, the region west of the Missouri River. Here the buffalo grazed in the greatest number. At this time the Indians pitched portable skin tipis and spent the days hunting, butchering, and drying meat for the winter ahead.

Hunting buffalo on foot required special skill. The

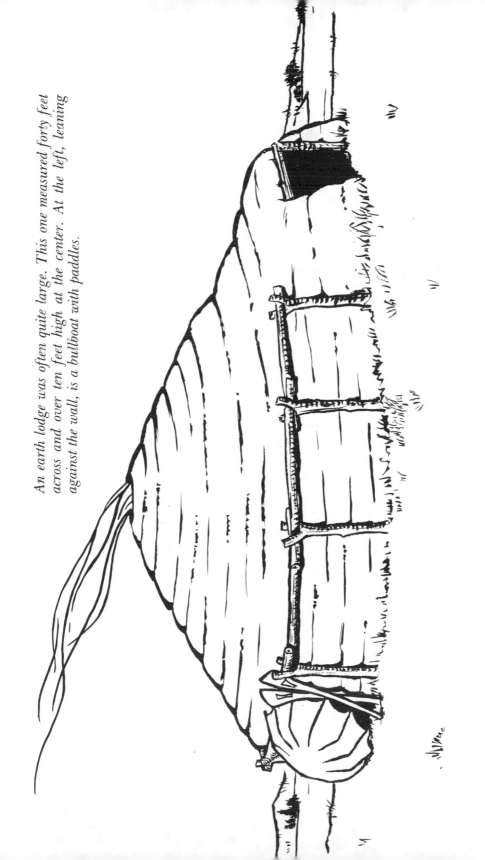

An earth lodge was often quite large. This one measured forty feet across and over ten feet high at the center. At the left, leaning against the wall, is a bullboat with paddles.

animals had poor eyesight, but their sense of smell was good. It was important to surprise them before human scent frightened them away. Men used to creep up to a herd disguised in animal heads and furs. Waving buffalo robes in the air, they stampeded the animals over a low cliff. Below, they had built a pen of branches and shrubs and, as the frightened beasts milled about, hunters closed in on them with bows and arrows. The beasts were skilled and butchered on the spot and loaded onto dogs, the only beasts of burden. Some of the dogs dragged a *travois (truh*-VOY), an A-shaped sledge made of two poles with a carrying net in between. But it was hard work carrying meat and skins back to camp.

Sometime after the year 1700, things changed. Through trade with southwestern neighbors, and through the ancient art of horse-stealing, the Plains Indians began to acquire horses.

According to a tale told by the Comanche, they were the first Indians to obtain the animals. When the first Spaniards arrived on horseback, the Comanche could not understand the "magic dogs." The lower part had four legs and ate grass. The upper part had two legs and ate meat. Then, of course, the Spaniards were recognized as men, though dressed in peculiar shiny skins and so pale underneath them that they must have been sick a long time. Some Comanche thought it would be smart to kill the men and keep their animals. But a wise man said, "You wouldn't know what to do with a magic dog if you had one. Follow the men when they leave here, and watch how they take care of the dogs." Which is just what the Comanche did. After spying for several days, they made off with two good specimens, and then nature took its course.

However the horses arrived, their coming led to a split among the Indians of the Plains. Some of the Indians continued to live along the rivers in the eastern Plains. Among these were the Mandan, Hidatsa, Pawnee, Arikara, Osage, and Omaha. Other Indians abandoned farming altogether and moved to the High Plains, where they lived as nomadic hunters. These are the Indians most famous in

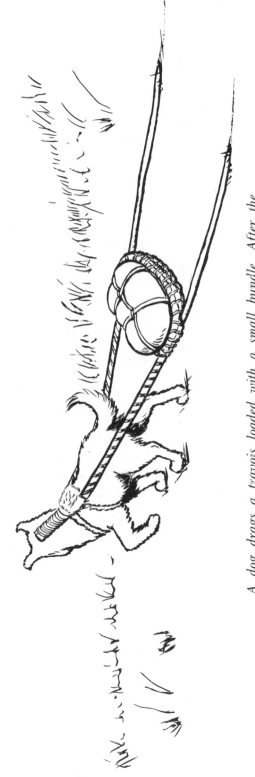

A dog drags a travois loaded with a small bundle. After the introduction of the horse on the Plains, Indians made a much larger style of travois for a horse to pull.

legend and history—the proud Cheyenne, Blackfoot, Crow, Arapaho, Kiowa, and Comanche. Perhaps the best known of all, the Sioux (or Dakota), had a foot in both camps, so to speak. Some bands remained in their original home, Minnesota, but most of them moved on to the High Plains.

In spite of this split, all the Plains tribes shared a number of characteristics. All of them depended to some extent on big-game hunting. Even for farmers like the Pawnee, meat formed at least half the diet. All of the Plains Indians lived at least part of the year in tipis. They were extremely warlike. And their lives were rich in ceremonies, from the individual sacrifices of a warrior such as White Hawk to great dances that brought together hundreds of participants.

Though there was one basic Plains culture, there were many Plains languages and language families. The Cheyenne and Arapaho spoke Algonkian languages. Siouan languages were spoken not only by the Dakota, but also by the Mandan, Crow, and Omaha. The Kiowa had their own language, and the Comanche had an entirely different one. Plains people worked out sign language as a useful solution to this problem. Through hand gestures, strangers could communicate a wide range of ideas, from "cold"—fists clenched, crossed on the chest, and trembling—to "peace"— hands clasped quietly together. Sign language was extensive enough to tell a long myth or to describe an encounter with an enemy.

Long ago, said an Arikara legend, buffaloes had a different form. They looked like strong human beings wearing horns, and they lived off the flesh of real people, which was stored on drying racks. These buffalo-creatures wanted to be turned into true animals, so a beautiful Buffalo Maiden taught a human hero, Cut-Nose, the magic that allowed him to do this. With special bows and arrows, Cut-Nose and other human hunters shot at the buffalo-creatures, who fled in a panic. Each buffalo-creature took a piece of stored human flesh along, tucking it under the armpit, and as the creature was shot, it turned into a true

In the midst of a herd of stampeding buffalo, Indian hunters kill their prey with spears and a bow and arrow. One daring brave, knife in hand, has leapt onto the back of a fleeing animal.

buffalo. Buffalo Maiden then married Cut-Nose. Their
children founded the Arikara nation, whose people had a
special magic for luring buffaloes. But whenever they killed
one of the animals, they left a portion uneaten under the
foreleg, since they believed it was human meat from their
ancestors.

Plains Indians did hunt and eat other game animals,
among them deer, elk, antelope, and bear. But the king of
the Plains, the hero of myths, and the very "staff of life" was
the buffalo. The first spring buffalo hunt was especially
important. In the winter, the herds moved away from the
High Plains. In the spring, sooner or later, they moved back.
No one knew for sure where the animals went, or when they
would return. If the buffalo returned late, the Indians were
in danger of starving. During the winter, all game was
scarce. People lived mainly on dried meat and roots, with
perhaps a little corn they had traded with farming Indians
who lived to the east. By springtime they were thin and
hungry.

If buffalo herds were nowhere to be found, shamans
sang songs and performed other rituals that had been
taught them by the spirits. Special women's organizations
staged dances to lure the animals near.

When a herd was sighted, the men readied their
"buffalo horses"—tough, fast ponies specially trained to run
alongside their quarry. No individual hunter was allowed to
go out on his own, for fear of frightening the herd away. If
anyone disobeyed, he was severely punished.

Riders surrounded a herd, then converged on it, using
both lances and bows and arrows. In later years, rifles were
used, too, but most Indians preferred a bow and arrow. A
good day's hunt might result in fifty slain animals.

The buffalo was of course used for food. A special
delicacy like the liver was eaten raw on the spot. Other
favorite parts, including the nose, the tongue, and the
hump, were eaten fresh. Much of the other meat was then
sliced and dried in the sun to make *jerky*. Another form of
preserved buffalo meat was *pemmican*, jerky pounded with
berries and mixed with melted fat and marrow. This was

The woman at left is scraping a buffalo hide to remove the hair. The flaps of the tipi, called "ears," could be adjusted to catch a breeze or keep out the rain.

"nutritious, but a pretty nasty dish until you got used to it," according to white people who tried it. (White Hawk and his men would have eaten mainly pemmican on their raiding expedition.) To make sausages, women filled the small intestine with chopped meat and roasted or boiled it. They made a sort of blood pudding by filling the buffalo's stomach with blood and cooking it over hot coals.

But, complete as it was, the buffalo was far more than a food supply. First, there was the hide. Women treated it by stretching it out on the ground, fur side down, and staking it flat to dry in the sun. They scraped away the fat and tissue until the surface was clean. Then they turned the hide over and removed the hair. The result was rawhide. It was strong enough to be used for shields. (Although the Indians relied as much on the effect of their painted designs and feather trimmings for protection as they did on the rawhide itself.) Buffalo hide was also stretched over a light wooden frame to make bullboats, the standard means of transportation on rivers of the Plains. Bullboats, being round, were clumsy. But they were so light that they could easily be carried by one person when a band was on the move. Rawhide was also used to make quivers, holders for medicine bundles, and boxlike containers for storing pemmican and other supplies.

Rawhide was stiff, and for many objects something more flexible was required. After women scraped and de-haired a hide, they tanned it by rubbing it with buffalo fat and brains, and smoothed it with a rock. The result was leather. It was used to make tipis, some clothing, moccasins, and soft pouches for holding tobacco, sewing equipment, or toilet articles. A buffalo hide tanned but with the fur left on made a warm robe to sleep on or bundle up in during the winter.

Apart from ritual sacrifices such as the portion the Arikara did not eat (and almost all Indians observed some similar prohibition), there was almost no part of the buffalo left unused. Bones were shaped into tools such as scrapers, awls, and needles. Arrow shafts might be straightened by drawing them through a perforated rib bone. Farming Indians used a buffalo shoulder blade as a hoe. Spongy, porous parts of the leg bone were used for painting decorations on rawhide and leather.

Buffalo sinew made strong cords for sewing and bowstrings. Indians drank out of buffalo-horn cups. They heated horns, hoofs, and shavings from the hide to make glue. A buffalo stomach was a good container for water, and for cooking by the hot-stone method. Some tribes even used the rough end of the tongue as a hairbrush. And, almost everywhere on the treeless Plains, buffalo droppings were gathered, dried, and burned as fuel.

Clearly the buffalo was as necessary to Plains life as the caribou was to life in the Subarctic. But Plains culture would never have developed its color, variety, and richness without another animal—the horse.

From the beginning, the Plains tribes were quick to see that the "magic dogs" would be an advantage to their way of life. Clearly, a man on horseback was a much better hunter than one on foot. Some of the southern Plains tribes may have had horses as early as 1640, but it took about a century for horses to spread in quantity throughout the Plains.

Horses became not only a means of living better, but also a sign of prestige. The more horses a man had, the more important he was. Every Plains Indian who wanted to amount to something needed at least a dozen horses, and it was not unusual for a tribal leader to have seventy or more. Obviously not even a large family needed so many horses just for riding or moving camp. But they were used as presents, as gifts to a bride's family, and simply for display. Even the size of a family's tent was determined by its wealth in horses. If it had many animals, there was enough transportation for a large tipi, which required as many as eighteen buffalo skins and many long poles for the framework.

Plains Indians learned to be excellent riders. They had simple equipment in the way of saddles, reins, and bridles. But a rider could cling to the side of a fast-riding pony and, as he galloped along furiously, draw a bow and shoot an arrow from below the horse's head, shielding himself behind the animal. Horses were treated with respect. Their owners talked to them like people, relating stories of brave horses in the past in order to inspire them. Unlike dogs, the other beasts of burden, they were hardly ever eaten except in case of famine.

Just as owning horses was a key to prestige, so was skill in hunting. A man who was good with the bow and arrow (or, later, the gun) was admired. When a boy could scarcely walk, he was given a bow and arrow and sent out to practice shooting. He was taught the habits of animals, how to set traps, and how to seek spiritual help in finding and killing game.

A boy started out by hunting small creatures, such as birds, squirrels, or skunks. Each new type of animal he killed he carried back to camp, where it was cooked and eaten with ceremony by his family and perhaps by other members of the band. The boy himself got none, but he did receive ample reward in the form of praise. Only when a youth had killed a big-game animal like a buffalo could he think of marrying and taking on an adult role in the community. Often his name might be changed in recognition of a particularly praiseworthy kill.

Hunting was hard work. It could be exciting, but it could also be dull, and hours of tracking in bad weather might bring no results. A long-time observer of the Cheyenne wrote, "Writers, quite ignorant of Indians, but who wish to give local color to fanciful descriptions of Indian hunting, sometimes describe the hunters as yelling in the excitement of the chase. It would be as fitting to write of a farmer as yelling in the excitement of plowing or of milking his cows."

What brought the greatest prestige to a Plains Indian— and prestige was far more important than possessions—was a raid against the enemy. This might be either a horse-stealing expedition or a revenge raid. In either case, the Indians preferred a short surprise attack, not a long campaign. There was no attempt to seize territory, though hunting rights were sometimes at issue.

From their childhood, boys on the Plains were taught to admire bravery and courage in the face of peril. Death was regarded with scorn, and danger was sought out deliberately.

One demonstration of bravery was the Plains custom of counting *coup*. (This is French for "a blow," or, more generally, a bold achievement.) For the Plains Indians, coup meant not only the achievement itself, but also bragging about it afterward—the "counting" part. The most important coup was touching the enemy on the field of battle with a lance, a special "coup stick," or, most impressive of all, with the hand. Various tribes had different rules about how many times coup could be counted on one person, usually twice or three times.

An Indian also counted coup when he touched a dead enemy, though this did not bring him as much credit as touching a live one. Again, the number of coups was limited to two or three, counted by the first two or three warriors to touch the body. Whites who observed several Indians racing toward a downed enemy and then scalping him thought that the scalp was the important goal, but it was not. Coup was the aim, and the scalp merely showed that there was one less enemy. (Women dried the scalps and carried them in certain dances and other celebrations.) Plains Indians sometimes took captives and occasionally tortured them, but this custom was not nearly as common with them as it was in the Woodlands and the Southeast. Most captives became servants.

Coup was counted when an Indian sneaked into the enemy's camp and stole a horse. For instance, Covers-His-Face would have counted coup on the horse he stole right outside the Crow tent. Hunters might also count coup on a good kill.

The actual counting of coup took place on ceremonial occasions, such as tribal get-togethers and initiation ceremonies. When exploits were first described, there might be lively arguments about who got credit for what. But after some discussion, with the older men refereeing, matters were usually straightened out to everybody's satisfaction. Plains Indians were not modest, but they were supposed to be absolutely truthful. Men often indicated coups by designs on their clothing and in the way they painted themselves. They also painted a visual record of their coups on tipis and buffalo skins. The skin records were displayed for admiration and also served as memory guides, since the Plains Indians had no other form of writing.

Plains men who were rich in horses and could count many coups were honored among their people. They could wear special headdresses, such as the great war bonnets made of eagle feathers. (Though these are the best-known Plains headdresses, there were other types, and one made of buffalo horns actually indicated greater prestige.) These men were the elite, the upper class. Sometimes they were what we would call "chiefs," sometimes not. For leadership was usually a temporary thing. A man seeking honor, like White Hawk, would get together a raiding party and lead it. If he was successful, he won respect. But someone else might well lead the next raid. No one man inherited power, and no one man had complete control over others.

During much of the year, Plains people lived in small bands of a hundred or less. They might all be related to each other in some way, and recognize a respected older man as their leader. But the leader had to consult most of the other men in the band before making any serious decision, such as moving camp. When a number of bands came together in the spring for a big buffalo hunt, the same spirit of democracy prevailed. About the only exceptions were the men who acted as policemen during group hunts. They did have power to enforce rules on their fellow tribesmen, but this was only for special occasions.

No matter what a person achieved on earth, everyone knew that it was due to help from the spirit world. Like most other North American Indians, the Plains tribes relied on dreams and visions as vital guideposts in the conduct of their lives.

Another spiritual aid was the sweat lodge. In many ways, this was the equivalent of the "Black Drink" of the Southeast, purifying the soul as it purified the body. Men built a special hut and piled heated stones in the center. When they poured water over these, clouds of steam

This Plains leader shows a blend of cultures. His moccasins, breechcloth, and headdress are Indian, but the cloth shirt and gun come from the whites. Note that over the shirt he wears an Indian breastplate and that he has added decorative designs to the rifle.

enveloped the people inside. The common practice was to make four waves of steam. (Four was a sacred number throughout North America.) Then the participants rushed outside for a dip in water, if there was some nearby, or, if it was winter, for a tumble in the snow. A Finnish *sauna* is very similar in principle. Some people think that the basic idea may have originated someplace in Asia and spread outward, both west and east. Warriors often had a sweat bath before they set out. If they had killed an enemy, they had another one when they came back.

The sweat lodge was also used before the most important of all Plains ceremonies, the Sun Dance. The name is not very accurate, since the ceremony did not honor the sun. However, during part of the ceremony, men did gaze for a long time at the sun.

The Sun Dance took place about once a year, when one man, the "pledger," announced that he had dreamed of the ceremony. It was conducted to gain additional spirit power—often to fulfill a vow made to the spirits in a time of distress. The Sun Dance was held most often in the spring or early summer, when the separate bands of a tribe assembled for the buffalo-hunting season.

First the "pledger" and a number of associates were instructed in the proper procedures by shamans. They learned the correct songs and other rituals for the ceremony, and were purified by a sweat bath. For several days they fasted. Then, when the first day of the dance dawned, they raised a big pole in the center of the camp. This was the focus of attention for the next four days. Among some tribes, self-torture was part of the Sun Dance. Certain men volunteered for this, in order to gain spiritual power and prestige. Holes were pierced in the muscles of their chests and backs. Through these, wooden skewers were run. Attached to the skewers were thongs suspended from the central pole. For four days, the dancers circled the pole with their eyes on the sun, praying and singing. A dancer constantly pulled back on the thongs that bound him. When the skewers had broken through his flesh to free him, he had fulfilled his obligation.

The Sun Dance was accompanied by many other ceremonies. There were dances held by women's societies, mock
battles between young men, and so on. Regular observance
of the Sun Dance was thought to make buffalo herds
multiply. It was both a solemn and a joyous occasion, and
served to give far-flung bands a sense of tribal unity.

The Sun Dance was only one of many Plains ceremonial
occasions. Every people had warrior societies, such as the Kit
Foxes of the Cheyenne. These societies not only preserved
order on hunts and in camp, but also staged dances on
special occasions. Indians who had been blessed by the same
animal guardian spirit—a grizzly bear, for example—might
form an organization and dance in imitation of the animal.
Men who owned especially sacred medicine bundles were
obliged to follow certain rituals, some of which were carried
out in public. A German traveler who visited the Blackfoot
in the 1830s commented on the activity in camp:

> Their ceremonies were without end—dances to bring the
> buffalo or to calm some spirit who had indicated dis-
> pleasure, seasonal observances that had to be made at the
> appointed time, private magic that required the coopera-
> tion of neighbors, fraternity rites, lodge meetings,
> prayers for love potions, commemoration of heroes.
> Town criers were always summoning emergency meet-
> ings for special situations. The normal death rate was
> always adding mourning shrieks to the noise. And some-
> one was always yelling and clattering rattles to scare
> diseases out of the sick.[1]

After their free days were over and they had settled on
reservations, many of the Plains Indians, looking back on
their life, thought its high point had come around 1850,
when game was plentiful and there were few whites. In
reality, however, the end had already begun, and by 1850
the Indians' days of roaming and fighting were almost
finished.

The whites began to come into the Plains in some

numbers in the early 1800s. Lewis and Clark crossed the northern part of the region on their exploring trip for President Jefferson in 1804–06. They, and other explorers who followed them, regarded the Plains as the "Great American Desert," unfit for white settlement.

There were plenty of furs, however. It was not long before white traders set up posts where they traded metal tools, guns, ammunition, and whisky to the Indians who brought in pelts. The effect on Indian culture was disastrous. The Mandan and Hidatsa were almost wiped out by a smallpox epidemic brought by white people in the 1830s. Some bands from other tribes pitched their tents around the trading posts and came to depend entirely on handouts from the traders. These Indians were known to the whites as "friendlies." All the others were considered "hostiles."

Not far behind the fur traders came travelers on their way farther west. Traders went southwest along the Santa Fe Trail. Pioneer settlers traveled to the Northwest along the Oregon Trail. The Indians resented their presence in Indian hunting lands, and often attacked wagon trains. Traffic increased after the discovery of gold in California in 1848 and other mining strikes in the mountains of Nevada and Colorado.

In the 1850s, the federal government began to make treaties with the Plains tribes. At the time the solution seemed fair. The government promised the Indians specified yearly payments. In return the Indians would not molest wagon trains and would allow military posts to be set up in their territory. But nobody thought very far ahead, and things quickly went wrong. Whites increased in numbers that alarmed the Indians. Indian agents in charge of payments cheated the tribes. Even when Indian agents were honest, Congress often failed to vote the necessary funds, so that the agents had to face the sullen Indians empty-handed.

The farming Indians of the Missouri River cooperated with the whites. The Pawnee, for example, gave up much of their land in 1857. Many of the men became scouts for the United States Army. The nomads of the High Plains, however, resisted long and hard.

Earlier, in the Southeast and in the Woodlands, troubled times had created strong Indian leaders—Osceola, "King" Philip, Tecumseh. The same thing happened on the Plains. Earlier there had been war chiefs only for a single raid. Now there were men known far and wide as leaders of proven bravery and strong "medicine"—men like the Sioux chiefs Sitting Bull and Crazy Horse. Even so, no one man could speak for all of the Plains Indians, or even all of one tribe. Whites might sign a treaty with, say, Red Cloud of the Sioux, regarding him as leader of all the Sioux. Then they would find that several Sioux bands continued to act as they pleased, since they did not regard Red Cloud as having spoken for them. There were many different bands of Sioux, but they were never united.

Things became worse after the Civil War. Soldiers went west to settle "the Indian problem." Veterans were looking for new land to farm. And people began to realize that the "Great American Desert," though dry, could grow crops. Now Indians were not asked simply to leave whites alone. They were assigned to reservation areas where they were expected to stay. These reservations were too small to support a hunting life. The Indians were supposed to become farmers. Said one Plains Indian:

> Once we were happy in our own country and we were seldom hungry, for then the two-leggeds and the four-leggeds lived together like relatives, and there was plenty for them and for us. But the whites came, and they have made little islands for us and other little islands for the four-leggeds, and always these islands are becoming smaller. Around them surges the gnawing flood of the whites, and it is dirty with lies and greed.[2]

The 1860s and 1870s were a period of turmoil and broken promises. In 1864 an eager colonel, J. M. Chivington, led troops that massacred a peaceful village of Cheyenne and Arapaho at Sand Creek, Colorado. (Severed arms and legs of the murdered Indians were later exhibited at a theater in Denver.) Indians in turn slaughtered white ranchers and burned lonely outposts. In 1868, Colonel George A. Custer, a Civil War hero, fell on the unsuspecting village of the Cheyenne Chief Black Kettle in Oklahoma. Custer's men gunned down women and children as they fled screaming from their tents.

There were men of moderation on both sides. Even among the Sioux, a chief could speak mildly as he dealt with whites negotiating for land west of the Missouri: "To whom does this land belong? I believe it belongs to me. If you, my brother, should ask me for it, I would not give it to you, for I like it and I hope you will listen to me." And even longtime Indian-fighters expressed a spirit of fairness. One of them said: "I have lived on this frontier fifty years and I have never yet known an instance in which war broke out with these tribes, that the tribes were not in the right."

But for every "friendly" there was a "hostile," or so it seemed. Men like Crazy Horse never signed a treaty. They vowed undying resistance to "Long Hair" Custer and all his kind. General Philip Sheridan believed that "the only good Indian is a dead Indian." And so the warring continued.

The whites had superior forces, backed by a strong central government, whereas the Indians were divided among themselves. Many had become totally dependent on food rations and liquor doled out by the whites. Worst of all, their mainstay, the buffalo, was disappearing.

The Indians themselves were partly responsible for the disappearance of the buffalo. With the guns they began using in the late 1800s, they destroyed more of these animals than ever before. But much worse were the white hide-hunters who descended on the Plains in the 1870s. At this time, Americans traveled about during the winter in sleighs or horsedrawn carriages and wagons, and used buffalo robes to keep warm. To supply the big market, professional hunters went west and shot down herds on a mass basis, stripping off the hides and leaving the animals where they lay. A Montana settler wrote about dead buffaloes he saw in 1880:

> In many places they lie thick on the ground, fat and meat not yet spoiled, all murdered for their hides, which are

piled like cord wood all along the way. 'Tis an awful sight. Such a waste of the finest meat in the world! Probably ten thousand buffalo have been killed in this vicinity this winter.[3]

The destruction of the buffalo was rapid, thoughtless, and almost completely effective. In 1850 there were some 20 million of them on the Plains. By 1889, when people finally got worried about what was happening, they counted a grand total of 551. Belated efforts were then made to preserve the buffalo from total extinction. Today sizable herds exist in both the United States and Canada.

At any rate, several bands of Indians gave up. As the saying went, they "came in," deciding to try reservation life. But many—the Cheyenne and Sioux especially—held out against the whites. The worst trouble came in the Black Hills of South Dakota and Wyoming, and in southern Montana. Here bitter fighting broke out when whites invaded hunting lands that had been promised to the Indians. Custer caused much of the trouble by issuing exaggerated reports about all the gold in the Black Hills. When the Sioux resisted the whites who flocked in, government troops were sent to subdue the Indians once and for all. It was then that Sitting Bull (more shaman than war chief) and Crazy Horse spurred their people on, shouting to the warriors as they set out on raids, "It's a good day to die!"

The climax came in June of 1876. Aided by Cheyenne allies, Sioux warriors played cat-and-mouse with a large army force along Yellowstone River in southeastern Montana. Both sides had their triumphs in small skirmishes. But the most stunning victory of all was that of the Indians over Custer. They trapped his force of some 225 men on a hillside near the Little Bighorn River. Every single white man in Custer's command lost his life.

"Custer's Last Stand" shocked and angered Americans, who could not bear the idea of "painted savages" holding the United States Army at bay. In the end, government forces prevailed. Sitting Bull and many of his people fled to Canada. Crazy Horse "came in" to an Indian agency in

Sioux warriors typical of those who fought Custer

Nebraska in May of 1877. With the 800 people and 1,700 horses he led, the procession was two miles long. As they neared the agency, the men began singing their war songs. Said one officer, "By God! This is a triumphal march, not a surrender!"

Surrender it was, no matter how it looked. The wild, free days of the proud riders were over. Maybe only the Plains Indians had the bravado to make a defeat seem like a victory.

7

"POOR STARVED DIVILS"

The Basin-Plateau

There are monuments to her along the route she followed—in Bismarck, North Dakota; in Three Forks and Armstead, Montana; and in Lewiston, Idaho. A mountain peak in northeastern Oregon bears her name. In Helena, Montana, a bronze sculpture shows her pointing the way for the two explorers, Meriwether Lewis and William Clark. She is Sacagawea, the famous Indian woman who guided the expedition that crossed the western United States in the early 1800s.

In the language of her people, the Shoshone, her name was Boinaiv, or "Grass Maiden". She had grown up among them in what is now Idaho. But when she was a young woman, her band camped for a time near the Three Forks of the Missouri River in western Montana. In a sudden raid, some Mandan Indians seized her and several Shoshone and carried them off to the Mandan village as slaves. This is when Sacagawea got the name by which we know her. (It may have meant "Bird Woman.")

Eventually Sacagawea married a French fur trapper named Toussaint Charbonneau. In the late fall of 1804, they were living in a Mandan village along the Missouri River, about where Bismarck, North Dakota, stands today. As winter was setting in, the Mandan were surprised to see three boats coming up the river, loaded with trade goods and manned by forty-five men. There were two leaders, Captain Lewis and Captain Clark. With them was a hand-picked force of frontiersmen and Clark's black slave, York. The Mandan were fairly used to white men, but York was a real curiosity. They clustered about him constantly, touching him and admiring his looks.

Lewis and Clark spent the winter at the Mandan village, sheltered from the snow and cold of the Plains. During that time, Sacagawea gave birth to a baby boy named Baptiste. When spring came, the exploring party was ready to move farther west along the Missouri. Their goal was the Pacific Ocean. Before they left, they hired Charbonneau as an interpreter, since he knew Indian languages. With him, wrote Lewis in the journal that both men kept, came "an Indian Woman wife to Charbono."[1] And with her, strapped to her back, was her baby.

That is the first mention of Sacagawea in the hundreds of entries that make up the journals of Lewis and Clark. References to her occur often, sometimes as "the Indian woman," sometimes by name. (This was usually spelled Sahcargarweah, though the two men, who agreed on most things, had different views about spelling.) Once, when one of the expedition's boats overturned, she rescued precious notes and scientific specimens that were in danger of being swept away by the current. Lewis noted at the Three Forks of the Missouri that this was the place where she had been captured. But he went on to say: "I cannot discover that she shews any immotion of sorrow in recollecting this event, or of joy in being again restored to her native country; if she has enough to eat and a few trinkets to wear I believe she would be perfectly content anywhere."

Apparently he had second thoughts a few months later, in August. Purely by chance, Sacagawea encountered her brother, whom she hadn't seen for years. "The meeting," wrote Lewis, "was really affecting." It was important for the explorers, too, since Sacagawea's brother was now leader of a band of Shoshone. These Indians were naturally more friendly toward a group that included a kinswoman than they would have been toward complete strangers. The Shoshone helped Lewis and Clark obtain horses and guided them across the rugged Bitterroot range of the Rocky Mountains.

When they first encountered Sacagawea's people, the whites had had luck in hunting and shot three deer. One was given to the Indians, who fell upon it and devoured it "nearly without cooking." Wrote Lewis: "I really did not until now think that human nature ever presented itself in a shape so nearly allyed to the brute creation. I viewed these poor starved divils with pity and compassion."

Sacagawea's help as a guide and interpreter was vital to the expedition, and worthy of being commemorated. But the journals contain many other references to her, too. Though less dramatic, they are very revealing.

Only two days after they left the Mandan village on the Missouri, Lewis wrote: "When we halted for dinner the squaw busied herself in searching for wild artichokes that the mice [probably gophers] collect and deposit in large hoards. This operation she performed by penetrating the earth with a sharp stick. Her labour soon proved successful, and she procured a great quantity of these roots."

By Christmas, the explorers had reached the Pacific coast and built a fort on the Oregon shore. After listing the "mockersons" and other gifts exchanged that day, Clark wrote: "We would have Spent this day the nativity of Christ in feasting, had we any thing either to raise our Sperits or even gratify our appetites. Our Diner concisted of porc Elk, so much Spoiled that we eate it thro' mear necessity, Some Spoiled pounded fish and a fiew roots."

Things were looking up on May 16, 1806, when the expedition was homeward bound. That day both captains made a point of mentioning Sacagawea's work. Clark wrote: "Shabonos Squar gathered a quantity of fenel [fennel] roots which we find very paliatiable and nurushing food." Two days later he described a group of Indians who "had been out several days and killed nothing. We gave them a small piece of meat which they told us they would reserve for their small children who was very hungary." One of the final mentions of Sacagawea was Clark's note in August 1806: "The Squaw brought me a large and well flavoured Goose berry of a rich crimsin colour."

Over and over the talk in the journals is of food. Often Sacagawea finds it. Often, too, we catch glimpses of people (whites as well as Indians) suffering from hunger. The Shoshone and their neighbors were poor people in a poor land. For them, a "fenel root" or a "Goose berry" could mean, literally, the difference between life and death.

The Shoshone (also called the Snake) belonged to a group often referred to as the Basin-Plateau culture. The home of these Indians lay between the Rockies on the east and the Cascade Mountains and Sierra Nevada on the west. Much of the land is wildly beautiful. It is also among the poorest in all of North America.

The Basin lies in the southern part of this region. It includes Nevada and most of Utah, a bit of eastern California, southern Idaho, and western Wyoming. The name is a good one, for the area is roundish and slopes upward toward its outer borders. Near its western edge is Death Valley, whose bottom point, over 280 feet below sea level, is the lowest spot in the Western Hemisphere. The hills and mountains that rim the Basin keep out rainfall, and the few rivers that cross the area do not flow to the sea, but disappear into swampy "sinks." Much of the region is a barren desert. Thousands of years ago, there were many lakes in the Basin, but most of them have evaporated. One that is still doing so is the Great Salt Lake of Utah. Summer temperatures in the Basin may reach 140 degrees Fahrenheit. But when the sun sinks, the night air can be very chill.

The Shoshone were Basin people. So were the Bannock, the Ute, and the Paiute. All of them spoke languages of the same family, related to that of the Hopi.

The Plateau, north of the Basin, is a high and fairly level tableland. It stretches from southeast British Columbia

This Nez Percé woman wears a fur robe and a basketry cap. The shelter is a blend of Plains (the tipi shape) and Basin-Plateau (the brush covering).

down through northern Idaho and eastern Washington and Oregon. Here the climate is less extreme than in the Basin, and two great rivers, the Columbia and the Snake, furnish life-giving water. The Plateau was the home of the Cayuse, Coeur d'Alene, Flathead, Nez Percé, and Shuswap peoples, among others. They spoke many different languages.

Farming was impossible in the Basin-Plateau area. Nor was there enough grass to feed large herds of buffalo. There was some hunting, though. On or near the Plateau, people might sometimes find deer, elk, mountain sheep, and game birds. In the big rivers there were salmon.

The sun-baked Basin offered much less animal life. Occasionally a herd of antelope might be found. Usually the Basin hunters had to make do with smaller "game," such as rabbits, birds, rats, mice, gophers, lizards, and snakes. Basin people also ate grasshoppers, locusts, ants, ant eggs, and fly larvae. These things are not very appealing to us, but tastes in food usually depend on what we're accustomed to eating. (When wagon trains first crossed Basin territory in the 1840s, whites gave the Indians sacks of flour and coffee. The Indians kept the sacks, but discarded the flour and coffee as inedible.) About the only creature the Basin people would *not* eat was the coyote. This was because it was thought to have some human qualities. In fact, according to a Paiute tale, the world had been created by Fox and Coyote singing and stomping in the sky.

Above all, the Basin-Plateau Indians were food *gatherers,* like Sacagawea. They picked wild berries and other fruits, gathered nuts and seeds, and dug up roots. Whites called many of the people "Diggers" because they always seemed to be poking away at the ground with sticks. On the Plateau grew the bitterroot plant, which, in spite of its name, had a root that was good to eat. There was also the camass, a kind of lily with an edible bulb. In the Basin, a staple food was provided by the pine nuts of the piñon tree. Altogether, Basin people ate the seeds, roots, or leaves of over a hundred different kinds of wild plants. The environment and the food supply of the Plateau made things a little easier

A man of the Basin "harvests" piñon nuts. The nuts, about a half inch long, have a sweet flavor.

there than in the Basin. But life for both groups of Indians were basically the same.

The Basin-Plateau offered few "raw materials" for survival. There were no logs for building, no birchbark for containers, no hides for shelter or clothing, no clay for pottery. Instead there was the scrub growth of dry lands— sagebrush, cactus, and thistles. So the resourceful Indians used these plants for all sorts of things. Their shelters, like the wickiups of the Apache, were crude huts of poles covered with brush or woven mats, easily thrown together and easily dismantled.

Women wove plant fibers into little aprons and string sandals, which was about all anybody wore in the summer. In cold weather, people kept warm with robes made of strips of rabbit fur. Plant fibers were also used to make sleeping mats and containers for cooking, using the hot-stone method. Women made such containers watertight by smearing them inside and out with pine gum.

When many people live on the verge of starvation, there is little time for anything but the search for food. This was as true for Basin-Plateau people as it was for the Subarctic Indians. Basin-Plateau Indians moved about a great deal, usually in small groups. Food could rarely be found in quantities large enough to support many people for any length of time. Little bands, like that of Sacagawea's family, ranged far and wide, for no one owned any particular territory. Often they moved on the advice of friends or relatives they encountered, who would tell them that deer had been seen to the north, or that rabbits were plentiful in a valley to the east. In the late fall, many bands went to piñon groves, where they collected thousands of ripe pine nuts. These were stored in pits to have on hand during the winter months.

From time to time, scattered bands would gather for a communal hunt of antelope, rabbits, game birds, or locusts. To catch antelope, Indians first built a corral of brush. Then they drove the animals into it and shot them. For rabbits and game birds, the Indians wove huge nets, some thirty feet wide, which they strung across ravines. They frightened

Boys close in on a pack of rabbits, driving them toward a pit where a man will club them.

their prey into the nets and then clubbed the animals to death. Locusts and grasshoppers were driven into trenches where fires roasted them alive. Some were eaten immediately, while others were ground into a kind of flour.

Group hunts were an occasion for feasting and socializing. The feasting was more or less a necessity, since these Indians did not know how to preserve meat. While they feasted, people who had not seen each other for months exchanged gossip and told stories. They gambled, raced, and held archery contests. They loved to dance, and men and women would sidestep in a huge circle for hours, singing all the time. In his journal, Lewis wrote of the Shoshone: "Notwithstanding the extreem poverty of these poor people they are very merry they danced again this evening until midnight."

Group hunts were also a time for young people to meet and marry. Family life was simple, with few regulations about whom one could or could not marry. (Most other Indian cultures had clans or other ways of tracing relationships, and many rules about marrying inside or outside the group.) In the Basin, where life was so hard, there were not always enough husbands and wives to go around. A man might have several wives or a woman several husbands. As in the Subarctic, when old people became too feeble to keep up with a moving band, they might be left behind to die. If times were desperate, newborn babies might be abandoned.

The Basin-Plateau peoples were extremely democratic, with practically no class distinctions. When a group hunt was underway, certain men—those who owned the rabbit nets, for example—directed the rest of the people. The nearest thing to a chief was an older man in the community who acted as a sort of clearinghouse for information about where and when various foods might be found.

The Basin-Plateau Indians did not have time for raiding and fighting like the tribes farther east. There was little theft and little quarreling. Murder might occur, usually when Plains Indians or the Apache raided their territory. But even then people didn't like to fight. Once when a Plateau village had been sacked, some hotheaded young relatives of those who had been killed wanted to go after the attackers. But an older man calmed them down, saying: "Our children are dead and our property is destroyed. We are sad. But can we bring our children to life or restore our property by killing other people? It is better not to fight. It can do no good." Revenge was a luxury to poor people.

Basin-Plateau people believed in the importance of a guardian spirit. In the Basin, people thought that spirits might appear in a person's dreams, but they did not try to bring about a vision by fasting or self-torture. It was different in the Plateau region, where all boys, and some girls, went out in search of a guardian spirit. People believed that, in adult life, a person's spirit reappeared to assert its power. When a man felt this about to happen, he invited people to a big Spirit Dance, where he sang, danced, and gave out gifts. The Spirit Dance was the only group religious ceremony of this area.

In the Basin-Plateau, as on the Plains, the first impact of the whites was felt when the horse was introduced. This happened in the mid-1700s. The horse was important to people who lived along the western edge of the Plains. With its arrival, some of the Ute, Bannock, and Shoshone, and most of the Nez Percé, took up a life of buffalo hunting. They learned to live in tipis, at least when they were out on the Plains. They made clothing of skins. Some even worked out their own form of Sun Dance.

In most of the Basin area, however, there was simply not enough pasture to support horses. Life went on as before. The very barrenness of the desert kept out whites for a long time. A few explorers, Kit Carson among them, passed through the area. Wagon trains rumbled across it occasionally. Then in the mid-1800s came the discovery of gold in California and silver in Nevada. Now more whites arrived and settled down. They and their animals destroyed much of the wild growth on which the Indians depended, so that many bands of Indians had to settle near white towns, begging for food. A few reservations were set aside, and the Indians moved onto these with practically no resistance. After all, they had little to lose.

On the Plateau it was not so simple. There were more whites, for one thing. After Lewis and Clark, fur trappers and traders arrived from both the United States and Canada. The Indians brought them furs in exchange for the usual guns, ammunition, and whisky. Through the fur traders, the Indians learned about Christianity. Actually they didn't learn from the traders themselves, who were hardly religious, but from their Iroquois helpers, who had been reared back east as Roman Catholics.

In 1831 a delegation of Nez Percé and Flathead went all the way to St. Louis to ask William Clark, who was by now governor of the Missouri Territory, for missionaries to come and teach them the ways of the new religion. Because the frontier was still unsettled and dangerous for whites, Clark turned them down. But five years later missionaries did come into the Plateau country. The best known, Marcus and Narcissa Whitman, settled among the Cayuse in Oregon. Some Indians converted. But many distrusted the white people's "medicine," which did not seem to be producing any more game than their own.

Meanwhile, the Oregon Trail had been opened, and pioneers streamed along it by the thousands to the lush valleys of the Oregon and Washington coast. They did not settle in the Plateau country, but their passage had its effects. For one thing, they brought measles with them. An epidemic among the Cayuse was so bad that they turned on the Whitmans, and in 1847, murdered all the whites in the mission.

More and more, the Indians seemed to stand in the way of white expansion. The hope of gold and silver brought miners to Idaho and western Washington in the 1850s. Railroads followed in their wake. Soon the tribes of the Plateau were placed on reservations, most of them peacefully.

The chief exception were the Nez Percé, who had enthusiastically taken up the roaming life of buffalo hunters.

A leader named Smohalla spoke for many hunting Indians when he explained to whites why his people could not become farmers or miners:

> My young men shall never work. Men who work cannot dream, and wisdom comes in dreams.
>
> You ask me to plow the ground. Shall I take a knife and tear my mother's breast? Then when I die she will not take me to her bosom to rest.
>
> You ask me to dig for stone. Shall I dig under her skin for bones? Then when I die I cannot enter her body to be born again?
>
> You ask me to cut grass and make hay and sell it, and be rich like white men. But how dare I cut off my mother's hair?[2]

It was a fellow Nez Percé, Chief Joseph, who led one of the most famous Indian "rebellions" in the United States. Joseph, like Sitting Bull, was more a spiritual than a military leader. He headed a band of some two hundred Indians in the beautiful Wallowa Valley of northeastern Oregon. Although some Nez Percé had signed treaties and settled on reservations, the majority had not. Joseph was one of these. For a while he and his people were left alone. In 1875, however, with whites pushing into the valley, the federal government ruled that Joseph must "come in" to a reservation in Idaho.

A deadline was set for early summer of 1877, and Joseph's band sadly prepared to give up. They journeyed to a resting place just outside the reservation. There trouble broke out. Angry young warriors killed some whites in revenge for the murder of a relative by a white man. When they fled south, they were followed by most of Joseph's band. Joseph wanted peace and was resigned to reservation life, but he felt that he could not desert his people. He joined them and helped in their successful defeat of a pursuing army unit. Then began an amazing flight.

Through hundreds of miles of wild flatlands and mountains, Joseph's people retreated, pursued by troops every step of the way. By this time other Indians had joined

Chief Joseph

his band. It now included about 200 fighting men, 550 women and children, and some 2,000 horses. Their goal was Canada and freedom.

The Indians trudged over the wild Bitterroot Mountains and through the Lolo Pass into Montana. The men, led by Joseph's younger brother, beat off attacks from other army troops who lay in wait along the way. On they went, through what is now Yellowstone National Park and north across Montana. They defeated another unit of federal troops at Canyon Creek on September 13.

By this time the whole country was watching the remarkable event in the Far West. Some Americans were outraged that United States Army troops should be "humiliated" by a band of Indians. Others cheered the courageous retreat of Joseph and his people.

The trip was long and hard, and there were many old people and young children. After the Indians' victory at Canyon Creek, they continued northward to within some thirty miles of the Canadian border. There they pitched their tents and rested. This was the fatal mistake.

On the last day of September, still another unit of federal troops, under Colonel Nelson Miles, caught up with the Nez Percé. In a pitched battle, many lost their lives, including Joseph's younger brother. Some Indians fled to Canada in small defenseless groups. The rest were besieged. The early winter of the northern Plains set in, and snow fell. After being promised a home at the Nez Percé reservation in Idaho, Joseph gave up. On October 4 he spoke, broken but dignified.

I am tired of fighting. Our chiefs are killed. The old men are all dead. It is the young men who say no and yes. He who led the young men [his brother] is dead. It is cold and we have no blankets. My people, some of them, have run away to the hills and have no blankets, no food. No one knows where they are—perhaps they are freezing to death. I want to have time to look for my children and see how many of them I can find. Maybe I shall find them among the dead. Hear me, my chiefs, I am tired. My

heart is sad and sick. From where the sun now stands I
will fight no more forever.[3]

Joseph kept his word. His captors did not. Instead of
sending him and his band to Idaho, the government
shipped them off to the hot plains of Oklahoma, where
many died. It was not until 1885 that Chief Joseph was
allowed to settle on a reservation in Washington. It was
near—but a world away from—his old homeland in the
Wallowa Valley.

8

PEOPLE OF THE POTLATCH

The Northwest Coast

The host and hostess stood waiting behind a curtain inside their new house. Everything was ready for the feast. Over their simple bark-cloth garments the couple wore beautiful fringed robes woven in white, black, blue, and yellow. The colors gleamed richly in the dim, windowless room. The host, Kinigwa, had tied his hair in a knot and painted his face with a single diagonal stripe. His wife, Statla, wore a large hat woven from spruce roots. She had painted her upper lip red in honor of the occasion.

The floor behind Kinigwa and Statla was piled high with many things. Most important was a "copper," a sheet of metal beaten out in shieldlike form and engraved with decorations. Behind it rose hundreds of blankets. And all around were cedar-bark mats, wooden dishes, spoons made of mountain-goat horn, and shell jewelry.

Nervously the host and hostess listened as their guests arrived. A relative of Statla stood just inside the door. He banged his staff on the floor at each new arrival, loudly calling out the guest's name. Ushers showed the guests to their seats on the wooden benches that stood along the sides of the house. Whispers and murmurs filled the air, especially as important chiefs and their families arrived. Everyone watched closely to see where newcomers were seated. Honored places went to men of highest rank, and rigid rules dictated the seating of every guest. It was a very formal, dignified reception.

Finally everyone had arrived. The curtain was thrown open to reveal the host and hostess and the piles of property behind them. As the guests applauded, Kinigwa and Statla strutted proudly back and forth in front of their goods. Then each made a speech. Statla told how she had gathered berries and preserved meat and fish. Kinigwa boasted of his great skill in wood carving. Now, having collected all the property, they were ready to part with it.

For this was the potlatch, the great giveaway feast of the Northwest Coast Indians. These Indians held potlatches on many important occasions, among them birth, marriage, and death. Kinigwa and Statla had just finished building a new house. That, too, was an occasion for a potlatch. But their feast was not simply a sort of reverse housewarming, with the hosts instead of the guests giving the presents. The most important part of this potlatch, as with all others, was the announcement of the host's new title.

Kinigwa had inherited his rank some years earlier, when his father died. But he had no official right to it until it had been formally witnessed at a potlatch. The same was true of a man who acquired a title in some other way, such as killing the man who had formerly held it. In each case, the new owner had to make his claim official with a lavish display of hospitality, which included bestowing gifts on many guests. A man won status not only by coming into possession of a title, but also by displaying his wealth. The two went hand in hand. Neither counted without the other.

Since Kinigwa's new rank obligated him to move into a big new house, he had held a house-building potlatch. Today was the last day of the ceremony, and the most important one. For days the guests had helped build the new house. This was the first time they had assembled in it as a group.

After he and his wife made their speeches, Kinigwa announced his "potlatch name," a long and complicated title that meant "Much Envied by All." This event was followed by the announcement of new names for the couple's four children. One by one they were brought forward, and their names shouted loudly so that everyone could hear them.

The father had inherited his name from his father. The children received new names because they had grown older. This was the way Northwest Indians recognized the many stages in a person's life. For example, a "baby" name was replaced by another name when a child first cut a tooth. That in turn was changed when a boy caught his first salmon or a girl first gathered berries.

All the names came from a stock "owned" by the clan, and had to be approved at a potlatch. Actually the names were really formal titles, used only on special occasions such as this one. "Everyday" names did not change.

Now came the time for the actual distribution of gifts. First went twenty blankets to each of the three most important chiefs there, men who had given house-building potlatches themselves. Then the men who had actually helped build Kinigwa's house were paid, also with blankets. Other blankets went to women who helped Statla when her children were born. Everyone, down to the smallest boy who had carried water for the house-builders, received at least one. Altogether, the host and hostess gave away almost a thousand blankets.

Kinigwa now stepped forward. From its place of honor he took the copper, which was so precious that it had a name—"Sea Lion." He held it up to be admired, and then ceremoniously presented it to Sigai. He was an important chief who had once given Kinigwa's father a copper. It was fitting to repay him this way. There was more applause.

Finally Statla and some of her relatives gave out the smaller gifts that stood ready. These were known as "trifles." When all the mats, dishes, spoons, and jewelry had been duly distributed, the guests left, carrying their gifts. These they deposited in a safe place until their departure later in the day.

When the people filed back, the food was ready. Women had spread out cedar-bark mats, and piled them high with clams, smoked salmon, and dried berries. Guests ate out of huge carved wooden bowls, eight people to a bowl. They dipped their fish into smaller dishes of oil. When they finished, they wiped their hands on "napkins" made of shredded cedar bark.

After the food was eaten, Kinigwa sang two special songs. He had inherited the right to sing these, along with his new title. His wife performed a dance, one to which her own rank entitled her. And then the potlatch was over. The guests picked up their gifts, loaded their canoes, and paddled home.

Kinigwa's potlatch had actually begun over a year earlier. It was then that he first announced he would give the feast. He loaned out many blankets to his relatives. They knew that they were to return twice that number in a year. This was why Kinigwa had been able to give away so many blankets.

Three months ago, Kinigwa had sent out messengers to extend formal invitations. Traveling by canoe, they stopped at many villages on the large island were Kinigwa lived. Altogether they invited over 300 people. When the guests arrived, they were given places to stay among the relatives of the host and hostess. Then, after the proper rituals had been performed, the men began the work of building Kinigwa's house.

First they went into the forest and cut down red cedar trees, which they floated back to Kinigwa's village. After stripping off branches and bark, they put up the main posts at the four corners of his house, and laid heavy beams across them. Then they hewed large planks. Some of these were fastened upright to the cross-beams to make walls. Others formed a roof.

Meanwhile specially honored guests were at work carving the great cedar trunk that would be placed at the front of Kinigwa's house. This was the totem pole. Like a coat of arms, it would symbolize the proud lineage of Kinigwa and his wife. At the bottom of the pole, the men carved a bear, crouching with his paws in front of him. Above him curled the tail and fins of a fish. At the top perched an eagle. He had a heavy down-curved beak, great oval eyes, and outstretched wings.

By the time the house was finished, the totem pole was ready. The men dug a big hole six feet deep. Near it lay the carved trunk, with pieces of wood under it. As some men lifted these, others pushed against the carved trunk with long poles. While raising the totem pole into the air, they slid it closer and closer to the hole. Finally they shoved it over the edge, and it fell to the bottom with a satisfying "chunk."

After the totem pole was up came the day of tattooing. That was when clan designs were applied to the children of the host and hostess, and to other village children whose parents paid for the privilege with blankets. It was a painful process. The tattooers took a needle and thread, rubbed the thread with soot, and "sewed" with it just under the surface of the skin.

It was time for Naka, the couple's youngest daughter, to have designs tattooed on the backs of her hands. She could not help crying at the pain. But the older children accepted what had to be done. After all, everyone who amounted to anything was covered with tattoos—not only on the backs of their hands, but also on their arms, chest, legs, the upper part of their feet, and sometimes even their cheeks. It sometimes took as many as six potlatches for all the designs to be completed.

Finally came the giveaway feast itself, when Kinigwa formally took upon himself his potlatch name. Every step of the month-long potlatch had its own special rituals. Most of them involved feasting, singing, and dancing. The potlatch was not an act of simple generosity. The guests were expected to repay their host within a year, either by giving him back a larger number of blankets than he had given them or by holding a potlatch themselves. Obviously the custom of potlatching was not for poor people living on the brink of starvation. It required enormous amounts of wealth. And wealth was just what the Northwest Indians had.

The Northwest Coast was a small but unique culture area in the far-western United States and Canada. It stretched from Yakutat Bay in southern Alaska down into what is now California. Thus it covered the coastal region of southern Alaska; all of eastern British Columbia, Washington, and Oregon; and a small portion of northern California. It extended eastward to the region of the Cascade Mountains. Toward the north, in Canada, the terrain was one of rugged mountains. Farther south, the hills sloped gently to the sea.

If you look at a map, you will see that this is an area of thousands of islands and inlets. It is a maritime region, meaning that it focuses on the sea. The climate is typically maritime, with water vapor rising from the ocean and condensing into almost constant rain and fog.

The major groups of the Northwest included the Tlingit, Haida, Tsimshian, Kwakiutl, Nootka, Coast Salish, and Chinook. The most distinctive things about the culture, such as the potlatch and the totem pole, were more common in the north than in the south. (The potlatch you just read about took place among the Haida, who lived on the Queen Charlotte Islands.)

The wealth of the Northwest Coast Indians was not in gold, rich land, or horses. They had two things in abundance—fish and wood.

The waters of the Northwest Coast, both the ocean and the rivers, teemed with fish. Salmon were most important. But there were many kinds of shellfish, plus ample supplies of halibut, cod, herring, smelt, and candlefish. This last fish got its name because it was so oily that, when dried with a wick inserted, it would burn like a candle.

In the sea lived quantities of marine game—hair seal, sea lion, sea otter, porpoise, and whale. There was land game, too. Indians who lived inland hunted deer, elk, and

Guests arrive for a potlatch. In front of the large wooden dwellings stand totem poles carved with mythical animals.

mountain goats. Like us, they valued beaver and other small animals for their fur.

One thing the Northwest Coast Indians lacked was farming land. Practically none of their territory was suitable for agriculture. In any case, fish and game were so plentiful that farming wasn't necessary. Women gathered berries and, in some places, the camass root. Otherwise their diet included no fruits or vegetables. It sounds monotonous, but apparently the women were inventive cooks. About the year 1900, a Kwakiutl woman was able to recite to an anthropologist 150 different recipes from her mental card file.

The other basic resource of the Northwest, wood, was as plentiful as food. Great forests of cedar grew down to the water's edge in many places. There were also groves of fir, pine, alder, yew, hemlock, and spruce.

The abundance of food did not mean simply that people had plenty to eat. It meant that they could live together in permanent villages instead of scattering in small nomadic bands to hunt game or wild plants. It meant too that the people were rich in traditions, social organization, and rituals. And it meant that there was leisure time, especially for the men. Women, as usual, were busy preserving and cooking food, caring for their children, and keeping house.

Leisure time was especially ample in the big salmon-hunting areas along such rivers as the Columbia and the Fraser. Salmon live most of their adult lives in the ocean. But when they are ready to spawn (lay eggs), they swim up into the rivers. At spawning time, in the spring, Indians would line the river banks and catch thousands of fish at a time. These could be smoked to provide enough food for months to come. So activity might be intense for a few weeks, but long periods would follow when men didn't need to work very hard.

Though the food supply was abundant, it still had to be caught. Northwest Coast peoples developed many clever fish traps, weirs, nets, and harpoons. To go after the big animals that swam offshore, they built beautiful, slim canoes. These

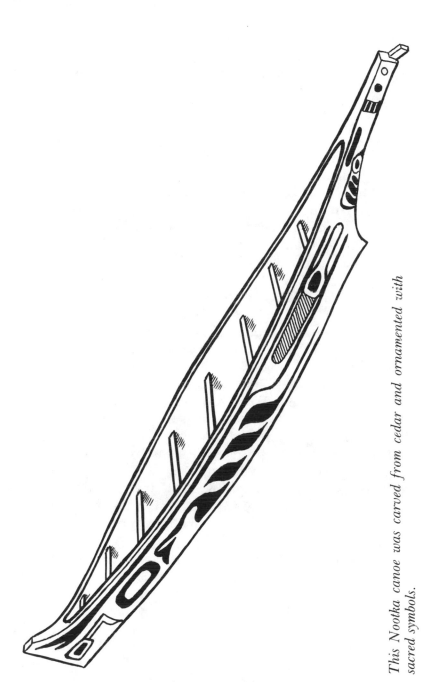

This Nootka canoe was carved from cedar and ornamented with sacred symbols.

they sanded down with sharkskin until they were as smooth as glass and could glide through the water with hardly a sound. The Haida were famous for their cedar dugout canoes, some over sixty feet long and eight feet across. The Nootka, too, made good canoes. These had an especially graceful curve from bow to stern, which some people think may have influenced New England clipper-ship builders. (New Englanders did begin to trade with the Northwest Coast Indians in the 1700s.)

The Nootka had another specialty—whale hunting. Only certain men could do it, for the tricks of the trade were handed down as family secrets. Some of these "trade secrets" involved how to make harpoons and lines and just where to throw them. Others had to do with magic rituals that would bring success. There were special charms, for instance, to make a whale swim close to shore, so that, after he was hit, he did not have to be dragged a long way. There were even rituals to bring to shore whales that had died of natural causes, so that the hunters did not need to go out at all.

Northwest Coast Indians dressed in a practical manner for the life they led. The climate was mild, so they didn't need heavy clothing. Women wove cedar bark into a kind of fabric. Out of this they made skirts for themselves and tunics for the men (though men often wore nothing at all). When it rained, the Indians protected themselves with bark-fiber rain capes and basketry hats. People who hunted deer and elk made some buckskin garments. Usually Northwest Coast Indians went barefoot. Since they were in and out of water a great deal, moccasins would have been uncomfortably wet most of the time.

Like most other Indians, the Northwest people had special garments for special occasions. Such were the ceremonial blankets worn by Kinigwa and his wife at their potlatch. Woven out of mountain-goat wool and cedar bark, they were made only among the Chilkat (a division of the Tlingit tribe), and other Indians traded for them. Some Chilkat blankets are still made, mostly for Indians to be buried in. Other ceremonial robes were made of bearskin or

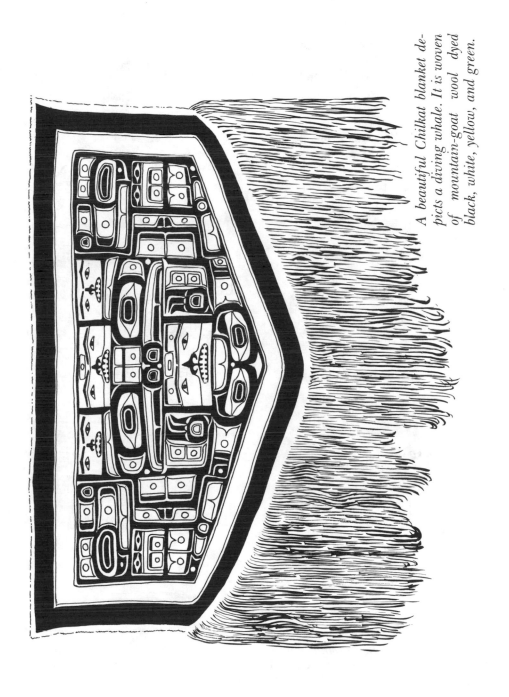

A beautiful Chilkat blanket depicts a diving whale. It is woven of mountain-goat wool dyed black, white, yellow, and green.

A Northwest couple are dressed in garments made of woven cedar bark. The man wears an ornament through his nose and a hat decorated with whales and fishermen. The woman's chin is tattooed.

fur. The Salish people raised a special breed of small dog whose hair they clipped for "wool."

Cedar-bark clothing was not particularly colorful, but Northwest people made up for it in several ways. Not only did they tattoo themselves, but they also painted their faces, and wore shell nose rings, necklaces, bracelets, and earrings. In addition, many women wore a labret—a piece of bone or shell inserted in the lower lip. Most Indians checked their appearance by looking in a still pool, if one were handy. But the Tsimshian actually made mirrors by smoothing a piece of slate over which they poured a film of water to reflect light.

Women made most of the clothing. They also wove cedar-bark mats to eat from, to sit on, and to sleep in. (The blankets given away at potlatches were worn mostly for show. After the coming of the whites, most of them were "trade blankets" obtained from the Hudson's Bay Company.) From cedar bark and spruce roots, women created beautiful baskets, some so tightly woven that they could hold water.

But it was the men who were the greatest artists. They were the ones with plenty of leisure time, and ample stores of wood to work with. Their tools were simple—adzes and chisels with cutting edges made of shell, bone, or iron. Apparently Northwest Coast people had iron before the whites arrived. It may have come from nails and other metal washed ashore on driftwood from ships wrecked at sea.

Northwest crafts are unusually beautiful. Men carved masks, drums, and animal figures for use at religious ceremonies. They steamed pieces of wood and bent them to form boxes, cradles, and backrests. They shaped graceful dishes and ladles for use at potlatch feasts. They produced excellent hunting equipment and fine canoes. They built large, sturdy houses and adorned them with totem poles and door posts.

Almost every one of these things was decorated with carved and painted designs. It is these designs that make Northwest Coast art so unusual. Once you have seen a few examples, you will always be able to recognize the culture from which they came.

The basic subjects used in decoration were animals, especially bears, eagles, ravens, wolves, whales, and fish. A clan used various combinations of animals to summarize its history. Each animal represented indicated that an ancestor had had a spirit encounter with it. (This is another example of the importance of visions to Indians everywhere.)

For us, it is often difficult to tell the animals apart. A carved box may look like a jumble of paws, beaks, and eyes, outlined in black and accented with red. The pattern is pleasing but unclear. Northwest Coast art was not representational, like the Plains skin paintings that depicted warriors' coups. Nor was it abstract, like the pottery decorations of the Southwest. It was conventionalized. That is, a few features of an animal were used to symbolize the whole thing. A short snout and protruding tongue stood for a bear, a long snout stood for a wolf, and so on.

Northwest Coast Indians liked symmetry, so in their designs they would often "split" an animal down the middle and open it out. They did not like empty space, so they would sometimes give an "X-ray view" by painting in the animal's bones. The dark wood and heavy black lines they used seem very appropriate to the Northwest setting of gloomy skies and dripping forests.

A family's house, furnishings, tools, and weapons not only displayed artistic taste and talent but also were meant to show how rich people were. Material possessions were very important to the Northwest Coast Indians. A poor person was not respected much, no matter how courageous or honest. But status did not come through possessions alone. It also came through rank, which was usually inherited.

The Northwest Coast people had chiefs. Below them was a long series of grades, each with its title and privileges. A man could move up the ladder. If he was a good warrior or canoe maker, the chief might bestow on him one of the higher titles that belonged to the clan.

Like the Southeast Indians, the Northwest tribes had

slaves. Usually they were taken in warfare. The villages from which they were seized could ransom them back, and often did. The menial chores slaves had to perform were bad enough. But much worse was the fact that their lives meant very little. Like any of their master's other possessions, they brought him prestige simply by existing. But if he were very rich, he could treat his possessions with contempt, and in that case, he might kill a slave. The Tlingit sometimes put a slave in the hole before they raised a totem pole, crushing him to death with its great weight. And the Kwakiutl sometimes killed slaves on the beach, using their bodies as rollers to bring a visiting chief's canoe on shore.

Captives were only a by-product of war, not the chief reason for fighting. Some Indians sent out fairly large war parties for what we would call tactical reasons. The Nootka and Kwakiutl went out in high-prowed war canoes to force rivals off fishing islands or other valuable territory. But small raids were much more common. If a chief died, some of his villagers might go out and kill the first person they met, to "send someone with the dead chief." They decapitated the body and put the head on display. (Northwest tribes did not do much scalping.) Feuds were frequent, too, but they were usually settled by payments rather than by physical revenge.

All in all, warfare was not so important for gaining prestige as it was on the Plains and farther east. The emphasis in the Northwest was on wealth and rank. And the potlatch combined these two things very well.

All potlatches involved rank and property. But the actual circumstances varied. Certain tribes paid a lot of attention to funeral potlatches, where a memorial totem would be set up to honor a dead chief. Other groups emphasized the giving of names to the children of the chief.

There were two unusual kinds of potlatches. One was the "face-saving potlatch." A man gave one of these when he felt that he had lost status and needed to regain it. He would do so if he had been captured as a slave and then ransomed. Or he might hold such a potlatch if he had tripped or committed some other social blunder at somebody else's potlatch. After his face-saving potlatch, no one could ever mention his mishap again.

The other special potlatch was the "competitive potlatch." It was held not simply to increase the giver's prestige, but to decrease that of his guests. (Once invited, people had to attend or be disgraced.) Kwakiutl chiefs were famous for such potlatches. They gave away thousands of blankets, and boasted to the skies. "I am the first of the tribes," a man would sing. Or "I am the great chief who makes people ashamed." A chief tried to give away so much that his rivals would bankrupt themselves in repaying him. As a further insult, he would destroy property. He might pour fish oil into the fire, tear apart blankets, chop up canoes, or kill a slave. There was even a special kind of weapon, shaped somewhat like a tomahawk, known as a "slave-killer." Needless to say, it was handsomely decorated with carved and painted designs.

The supreme act of arrogance at a competitive potlatch was to destroy a copper. A chief might throw it into a fire or over a cliff. Or he might break off pieces and contemptuously hand them out to his rivals. All the time he and his family would praise his wealth and belittle that of his rivals.

The whites who began moving into the Northwest in the late 1700s disapproved of the potlatch. It seemed wasteful to them, and they thought it took the food out of children's mouths. One white wrote this report about the Kwakiutl: "Their chief aim is to go through life easily and get all the fun and glory they can out of it. The glory comes from giving a potlatch, the fun in doing nothing as often as possible."

Actually, in this economy of abundance, few people went hungry. And a potlatch was a more humane way to beat a rival than the raiding expeditions and tortures of other Indians. The Kwakiutl themselves recognized this. In the old days they had fought with other Indians, but gave up warfare in the 1800s. They referred to their potlatches as

This fine Haida copper measures almost a yard high. The engraving below, typical of Northwest Coast art, shows an animal "split" into two symmetrical halves.

"fighting with property." There are worse ways of fighting.

Potlatches were often occasions for elaborate ceremonies staged by shamans and dance societies. The Nootka and Kwakiutl were known for these. The basic idea was always the same. A villager was kidnaped by a supernatural being. He was held captive for a time, during which he received supernatural powers himself. Then he returned to show off what he had learned.

The actual "kidnaping" took place when a man slipped quietly out of his village one day, or else was carried off by people wearing strange disguises. He stayed in hiding for a while. When he returned, he usually chose an evening for his performance, since it looked doubly impressive at night. Depending on the spirit that inspired him, the man danced or performed magic tricks.

These performances, held indoors by flickering firelight, were spectacular shows. The chief actor and other performers wore elaborate costumes with great carved masks. Many of the masks were jointed. An actor might dance for a while as a wolf. Then he would pull a string and his mask would open to reveal, inside, the head of an eagle. Under his costume a performer might carry an animal stomach or bladder filled with blood. If he was "stabbed," the blood gushed forth realistically. Actors and puppets swung through the air on ropes strung across the ceiling. After crawling along an underground tunnel, an actor might suddenly spring out through a trapdoor. Or, using hollow stems buried under the floor, he could make his voice suddenly seem to speak out of a fire.

A few white explorers traveled along the Northwest Coast as early as the 1740s. But the first important contact between whites and Indians of the area came when Captain James Cook explored Nootka Sound in 1778 on his way to Alaska. Soon afterward, a busy three-cornered trade sprang up. English and American sea captains anchored offshore and traded metal tools and weapons with the Northwest Coast Indians for sea-otter pelts. These they took to China,

This hinged Kwakiutl carving is a mask within a mask. The wearer could open or close it it as he danced.

where they were in great demand as trimming for robes. Then the ships went back to England or the east coast with porcelain, tea, and silk.

Sea otters became harder and harder to find, but there were plenty of other furs in the area. In the early 1800s, trading companies set up posts at strategic places. Most important were the Hudson's Bay Company posts in British Columbia. Relations between traders and Indians in Canada were generally good. The traders left the Indians alone, although they did try to outlaw the potlatch. There were few settlers to move in on their lands, and the Indians were not put on reservations.

In the United States the land was more attractive to settlement. Pioneers began arriving over the Oregon Trail in the early 1840s. Once more it was the old story. Indians held the land the whites wanted, so the whites decided to move the Indians to reservations. This happened in 1854. Some groups refused to go, and fought a number of small and hopeless "wars." And some families simply stayed on among the whites, intermarried, and eventually lost their Indian identity.

Although official policy differed in Canada and the United States, one factor was the same. With them, the whites brought diseases that devastated the Indian population. Thousands died from measles, smallpox, and tuberculosis. Some of their former customs had protected them from certain illnesses, even though they didn't know it. In wet weather, for example, people who went inside usually took off all their clothes. The whites, however, taught them to be ashamed of nakedness. So they kept on their wet clothes and became more subject than before to pneumonia, bronchitis, and influenza.

It wasn't until the 1900s that the Indians began to develop resistance to white diseases. The danger of complete extermination had passed. But there were not many people left to carry on the old traditions.

9

THE LAST OF THEIR KIND

The Indians of California

White people gave him the name "Ishi," which simply meant "man" in his own language. They never knew his real name, for he never told them. But at least he no longer had to be called "the Wild Indian."

When Ishi stumbled into the little town of Oroville, California, in 1911, he caused as great a stir as if he had swooped down from the hills waving a tomahawk. Not that there were no Indians in California. But they lived on reservations or among the whites. There were no bands still roaming free. Or so people thought, until Ishi was found one early August morning, half naked and crouching fearfully against a fence, kept at bay by a pack of dogs.

Ishi could not speak English, but it was obvious that he was exhausted and very hungry. The sheriff put him in the county jail, since there was no place else to protect him from curious onlookers. He was given clothes and food, though for several days he seemed too terrified to eat much. Indians and half-breeds from the community came to try to talk to him, but none of the languages they tried worked.

Then anthropologists at the University of California heard about what had happened. They thought they knew what tribe Ishi belonged to. Word lists in hand, one of them, T. T. Waterman, went immediately to Oroville to talk to the "wild Indian." He could, though not perfectly, since Ishi's dialect was somewhat different from those recorded by the anthropologists.

Ishi did not spill out his story in a gush of words. Even if there had been no language barrier between him and Waterman, he would not have done so. He was a shy man. And the events of his life, especially in the previous few years, were painful for him to recall. In fact, he was never able to talk about them in detail.

Ishi went to live at the University of California anthropological museum, which at that time was in San Francisco. (He was also given a choice of remaining in the hills from which he had come, or of settling on a reservation, but he didn't want to do either.) In San Francisco, he became a sort of ward of Waterman's and of a famous California anthropologist, Alfred L. Kroeber. The two men became his friends, known to him as "Watamany" and "the Chiep" (chief). To them, over the four and a half years that remained of his life, he told his story.

As nearly as could be figured out, Ishi had been born around 1862. He belonged to a group known as the Yahi, which was part of a larger California tribe, the Yana. The Yana probably numbered about 3,000 at their peak. They lived in northern California, near Mount Lassen. In this region of forests and deep gorges, they hunted and gathered wild plants. In the old days, it had been an uncertain life but a good one.

By Ishi's time, however, the good life was over. During the Spanish and Mexican occupation of California, mountain (or "wild") Indians like the Yana had been left alone. But after the coming of the Americans in the 1840s, things changed. Many more whites came into the state, and they settled almost everywhere. Though they did not move directly into Yana territory, they lived near it. Their animals atc the wild plants on which the Yana lived, and their mining operations polluted the streams. The Indians raided the whites from time to time, mostly out of hunger and fear.

Some Indians west and south of the Yana were rounded up and sent out of the area. But the Yana and many other "wild" Indians avoided white contact. White Californians (not the federal government) decided to wage all-out war against them. Their aim was nothing less than extermination, and they were very successful. In the 1860s and early 1870s, posses of white men rode throughout the hills and killed Indians wherever they found them—alone, in small groups, sometimes whole villages. Waterman took down this account many years later:

> A party of whites, in April of 1871, pursued a band of Indians with dogs. They located them in a cave across a narrow gulch, and shot a number of them, finally entering the cave itself. Here they found a lot of dried meat, and some small children. The hero of the occasion, being a humane man, a person of fine sensibilities and delicacy of feeling, could not bear to kill these babies—at any rate, not with the heavy 56-caliber Spencer rifle he was carrying. "It tore them up too bad." So he shot them with his 38-caliber Smith Wesson revolver.[1]

By 1872, when Ishi was ten, there were hardly any Yana left. His own group, the Yahi, apparently numbered twelve or thirteen. Because they knew their hill country so well, they managed to escape the whites who still rode through it from time to time. They kept their fires small so as not to attract attention. Occasionally a white would see one of them fleeing through the woods.

Over the years their number dwindled. In November 1908 a group of white men stumbled across the tiny village where Ishi lived. By this time, there were only four Yahi left. Except for Ishi's mother, who was too weak and old, they fled into the woods. The whites did not harm the old woman, though they took every bit of dried food the Indians had as provisions. Ishi returned to his mother. His two companions were never heard of again. Possibly they drowned, or fell to their deaths in one of the many gorges. Ishi's mother apparently died a few days or weeks later. For the next three years, Ishi lived in the woods totally alone. In the end, sheer loneliness must have combined with hunger to overcome his fears and drive him down from the hills into a community of the hated whites.

When he went to San Francisco, Ishi was about fifty years old. He lived in a comfortable room in the museum and earned the small amount of pocket money he needed by working there as a janitor. He could come and go as he pleased. He enjoyed visiting people and walking and riding around the city, especially after he learned some English. He spent a lot of time with the anthropologists, recording his language and showing them the traditions of his people. He also gave public demonstrations of such crafts as arrow-making.

As a person, Ishi was neat, cheerful, and reserved. The great inventions of the white world—bridges, airplanes, and tall buildings—impressed him less than the small ones—running water, window shades, matches, and glue. He never got over a fear of crowds. For reasons never quite under-stood, door knobs, safety pins, and typewriters struck him as funny. He liked most white men and admired their clever-ness, but it was obvious that he sometimes found them noisy, ill-mannered, and lacking in a true understanding of nature. He died of tuberculosis in 1916. Saxton Pope, his doctor and long-time friend, wrote after his death:

> And so, stoic and unafraid, departed the last wild Indian of America. He closes a chapter in history. He looked upon us as sophisticated children—smart, but not wise. We knew many things, and much that is false. He knew nature, which is always true. His were the qualities of character that last forever. He was kind; he had courage and self-restraint, and though all had been taken from him, there was no bitterness in his heart. His soul was that of a child, his mind that of a philosopher.[2]

Ishi's story is unique. And yet it tells us much about his

*In 1914 Ishi and some of his anthropological friends journeyed back
to his homeland. He showed them, among other things, how he used
a harpoon to fish for salmon.*

culture, and gives us insight into a people now largely vanished.

The Indians of California formed their own culture area, the smallest in North America. Actually, it did not even include the whole state. A small portion in the north is considered part of the Northwest, and another small portion in the east is part of the Basin.

California Indians were hunters and gatherers who lived well. The population of the area was dense, at least for Indian America. Over 125,000 Indians lived in California when whites arrived—probably more than in any other North American culture area. And they formed more different groups speaking more different languages than any other region in all of Indian America. There were some 40 major groups, with names unfamiliar to most of us: Modoc, Shasta, Pomo, Yana, Chumash, Wintun, Maidu, Miwok, and Yokuts. These in turn were divided into almost 500 smaller groups known as "tribelets." The Yahi were a tribelet.

The California Indians spoke over a hundred different languages belonging to distinct language families. No wonder Ishi had trouble talking even to Batwi, a reservation Yana whose original home lay north of Yahi territory. As a matter of fact, Batwi and Ishi never did get along well. Batwi looked down on Ishi, while Ishi regarded Batwi as a "phony white man."

Like the Basin-Plateau people, the California Indians ate almost everything they could get their hands on. If they lived near streams, they speared salmon. If they lived near the ocean, they caught shellfish. In the mountains they shot deer. Nor did they shrink from eating earthworms, grasshoppers, and caterpillars. Women gathered a great variety of ferns, roots, nuts, berries, and seeds. People liked wild waterfowl too. Men caught these by floating among them with their heads hidden by gourds. Then they would reach out and snatch the birds by their feet as they swam by.

Waterman wrote to Kroeber after one of his first interviews with Ishi: "We had a lot of conversation this morning about making acorn soup." Acorns were the basic food of the California Indians. They grew almost everywhere, and could be stored a long time. The remarkable thing is that most kinds contain an acid, tannin, that makes them impossibly bitter to eat in their natural state. Somehow, over the centuries, Indians figured out how to solve this problem. First the acorns were shelled and dried. Then women ground them between stones. They got rid of the bitterness by pouring water over the kernels so that the tannic acid was filtered out through beds of sand or tightly woven baskets. After that came drying, roasting, and a final grinding. The result was a nutritious flour that could be made into a sticky mush or a kind of flat bread.

As might be expected in the warm climate of California, clothing and shelters were simple. Men commonly wore nothing at all, except maybe a buckskin breechcloth. Women wore small double aprons of bark fiber and brimless hats that were really little upside-down baskets. In cold weather, such as the Yana had in their hills, people wore fur cloaks and sandals of grass or buckskin.

Most Californians lived in small domed houses made with bunches of grass or rushes tied onto a framework of bent poles. Men made more substantial structures, covered with earth, for use as sweat lodges. These served as clubhouses, too, and young unmarried men often slept there.

The craft on which the Californians lavished most care and achieved the most notable results was basketry. Men used roots, bark, and reeds to make basketry fish weirs, coarse storage containers, and baby carriers. But it was the women who did the finest work. They wove containers of all shapes for carrying, storing, cooking, and eating. In size these varied from a few inches to many feet in diameter. They were decorated with pleasing abstract designs and often adorned with feathers and shell beads. The Pomo, considered the greatest of all Indian basketmakers, produced some baskets so fine that a microscope is needed to count the individual coils. The Pomo had a special belief about patterns of horizontal bands. A horizontal band was

A Hupa woman weaves a large basket. Her husband, dressed in a fur robe, carries a wide, flat bow typical of the California Indians. Backed with sinew, it was very strong.

never completed all the way around, but was left with a break. Only this way could the maker avoid being afflicted with blindness.

Although California Indians scattered in small groups during the spring and summer, they often came together to live in villages during the winter. Chiefs and their families were the most important village members, and there might be additional officials, such as directors of rituals. Ishi's name for Kroeber indicated the respect he and his people had for rank.

As in so many other areas, peace chiefs were not the same as war chiefs. Among the Californians, war was not important for plunder or as a way to gain honor. They did fight for revenge, and to guard their small pockets of territory from interlopers. It was common for two warring tribelets to meet and line up facing each other. Then each would send out a single champion to fight. Like a medieval joust, this sort of contest was a pleasure for the spectators and satisfied wounded pride, too.

In another early letter to Kroeber, Waterman wrote about Ishi: "If I'm not mistaken, he's full of religion— bathing at sunrise, putting out pinches of tobacco when the lightning strikes, etc." That was true, though Waterman expressed it rather clumsily. For Ishi, as for almost all Indians, the world of humans, nature, and spirit were one. His friend Dr. Pope first won his respect as a doctor not for his surgery but because he knew some magic tricks. Thus he proved himself a good *kuwi*, a shaman.

One organization of the California Indians was especially aimed at bringing individuals into closer contact with the spirit world. This was the *toloache* (TOLL-*wha-chee*) cult. Its main feature was the drug Datura, or jimsonweed. (The latter name comes from "Jamestown," where early settlers cooked and ate the leaves without realizing what would happen. Unlike the Indians, they didn't make a habit of it.) Young people, supervised by their elders, drank a mixture of Datura leaves, stems, and roots pounded and soaked in water. It produced visions that brought them spirit helpers, foretold the future, and helped them see things that would otherwise be hidden.

Another society widespread in California was like the kachina cults of the Southwest. This was the *Kuksu* cult. Like kachina dancers, men initiated into the Kuksu cult danced in costumes to impersonate various animal spirits. Kuksu was the most important of these. Children were taught to believe that the dancers really *were* the spirits. Only after they were initiated did they learn that fellow tribesmen danced in disguise. As in the Southwest, people nevertheless believed that the real spirits were somehow present, too.

When Ishi first stumbled into Oroville, his hair was cut short. This was a sign of mourning, probably for his mother. (Most California Indians wore their hair long.) Even in his solitary state, Ishi preserved proper behavior in re-membrance of the dead. Death and beliefs about it were extremely important to the Californians.

When death did come, elaborate measures were taken to help the spirits of the dead rest in peace and to prevent the return of their ghosts. The name of the dead person was not spoken, sometimes for a year, sometimes longer. (Ishi never revealed the name of his mother.) Often the dead person's house and possessions were burned. Close relatives cropped their hair and often covered their heads with pitch.

Among many tribes, big ceremonials were held annually in memory of the people who had died during the previous year. Mourners danced around a great fire, flinging clothing and other property into it to supply the dead. A white journalist described an impressive ceremony among a Yokuts tribelet in the 1870s:

> The blaze of the sacred fire flamed redly out between the bodies of the dancers, swaying together. The disheveled hair of the leaping women wildly snapping in the night wind, the bloodcurdling rasp of their breath, and the frightful writhings of the mourners, produced a terrible effect. At the sight of this weird spectacle, I felt all the blood creep and tingle in my veins, and my eyes moisten with the tears of a nameless awe and terror. We were beholding, at last, the great dance for the dead.[3]

Although explorers claimed California for Spain as early as 1542, the region was not colonized for a long time. Franciscan friars from Spain's colony of Mexico established the first mission, at San Diego, in 1769. By 1823, the friars had built twenty-one missions in California, each about a day's walk from the next.

One of the primary aims of the missions was to convert the California Indians to Christianity. For this purpose the friars encouraged tribelets to settle down nearby where they could be taught the arts of civilization. Often the "encouragement" amounted to forcible roundups and the "teaching" to virtual slavery.

About 25,000 California Indians settled at the missions, and became known as Mission Indians. Some apparently adapted well. A visitor to Santa Barbara wrote of the Chumash Indians there. They formed an orchestra, were singing with "elegance," and were industrious at work and "of good appearance, with an affable manner." On the whole, Mission Indians worked very hard, and were punished if they tried to escape.

One thing was certain. No matter how they fared as converts to Catholicism and civilization, the Mission Indians died in great numbers from new diseases, among them pneumonia, measles, smallpox, and tuberculosis. Even those who lived faced an unhappy fate. The missions were abandoned in 1834 when Mexico, by now independent, sold them to private owners. After that the Mission Indians were on their own, with no one to guide them or help them; the friars had at least done that. Most Mission Indians lost all will to survive. Entire tribes vanished, with even their names forgotten. According to one estimate, nine-tenths of the Mission Indians were dead by 1849.

For the "wild" tribes like the Yana, life was not disrupted until the arrival of gold-hungry Forty-Niners. But occupation by the Americans was worse than that of the Spanish and Mexicans. The Spanish and Mexicans had wanted to help the Indians. The Americans had no such interest. Even though the government negotiated several treaties with California Indians in 1851 and 1852, the

United States Senate yielded to pressure from land-hungry California whites and refused to ratify the treaties.

The Indians had literally no place to go. Many were kidnaped and sold into slavery. A clergyman in Los Angeles in 1855 reported that he saw an Indian girl lying in a dying state by a wall, tended by an old couple who were apparently her parents. He learned that the man who owned her, when he found out she was dying, "to avoid the expense of her burial put her in a cart and took her down there and unloaded her by the side of the road."

Many "wild" groups, like the Yana, were simply hunted down and wiped out. According to an official estimate by the Bureau of Indian Affairs, the 100,000 "wild" Indians in 1851 had been reduced to about 17,000 in 1890. Those that remained were described as "broken down in spirit, demoralized, and indolent, but perfectly docile and harmless, depending mainly upon the charities of the white people."

By the early 1900s the white Californians, thoroughly in control, could finally afford to show some compassion for the Indians who still lived among them. They set aside about a hundred reservations and rancherias. (The latter are small plots of land, sometimes no bigger than two acres.) Ishi probably made a wise choice in refusing to settle among these degraded members of his own race. He died of a disease "imported" by whites, but at least he died with dignity.

10
RESERVATIONS AND AFTER

When the United States was a young nation, George Washington promised a group of Seneca Indians that "the General Government will never consent to your being defrauded, but will protect you in all your just rights." Almost two hundred years later, the "General Government" was still trying to prevent Indians from being cheated and to protect their rights. It wasn't easy.

Just about everyone would agree that Indians have been cheated, hundreds and thousands of times. For this reason, and others as well, American Indians today are one of the most unfortunate of all minority groups. They are poor. Among Indians, the average family earns only about half the average family income of the United States as a whole. Indian unemployment is at least seven times higher than that among other Americans. Indian health problems are many. Indian babies die at birth in greater numbers than other American children. The average non-Indian American can expect to live to the age of seventy, while the average Indian will die before fifty. Despair and hopelessness are common. Alcoholism afflicts one in three Indians, and the suicide rate is twice what it is for the entire United States population.

Many Americans know about these depressing facts, and a lot of people—not just Indians—would like to do something about them. Since the formation of the United States in 1789, there have been almost 400 treaties with the Indians. Congress has passed over 5,000 laws concerning Indians. Federal court judges have handed down some 2,000 decisions interpreting the treaties and the laws. The United States has had at least five different major policies for solving the "Indian problem." Indians have formed many different organizations with many different aims. Nothing has worked.

Not too long ago, many Americans thought that the "Indian problem" would cure itself rather easily. There simply would not *be* any more of them. It was certainly true that, for many years, the Indian population declined steadily. In 1492 there may have been about a million Indians in what became the United States. Wars and disease took a huge toll. In 1870 the Census Bureau counted only some 25,000 "vanishing Americans." That was the lowest point. From then on, to many people's surprise, the figure increased. Most of the wars were over. Indians had developed resistance to many "white" diseases. Year after year, their numbers grew. Today, there are about 1 million Indians in the United States. Canada has about 300,000.

Statistics like this are only approximate, since no one is sure what an Indian *is*. Generally, he or she is defined as a person with at least one Indian grandparent—that is, with at least one-fourth Indian "blood." But, in some cases, people with mostly white "blood" may live on reservations and consider themselves Indians. At the same time full-blooded Indians may live among whites and think of themselves as whites, especially if they want to avoid discrimination. Even the United States government does not have a single official definition of an Indian.

This confusion reflects the bewilderment most of us feel about Indians today. How do they live? What are they like? What do they want? The bewilderment is nothing new. In fact, it started with Columbus.

On his first journey to America, Columbus paid special attention to the people he discovered and named. He found them both "incurably timid" and "artless and generous." And he said: "Of anything they have, if it be asked for, they never say no, but do rather invite the person to accept it, and show as much lovingness as though they would give their hearts." This generosity was repaid by enslavement and extermination. Of course there were humane Spaniards, especially among the missionaries. They wanted to save not only the Indians' souls, but their bodies as well. Because of their urging, the Spanish passed laws in an attempt to protect Indians from the worst forms of cruelty and mistreatment.

One thing the Spaniards were certain about. The Indians were defeated peoples. They had no rights of their own other than what the Spaniards gave them. Millions of Indians in Latin America were put to work for their conquerors, with whom they lived. Over the years, Indians and whites intermarried in great numbers. Today, in countries such as Mexico, 90 percent of the people have at least some Indian "blood."

In Canada, the Indian population was small, probably under 200,000. There were few outbreaks to subdue, and neither the French nor the English made a practice of Indian slavery. The French especially had a tolerant attitude toward the Indians. Many Frenchmen married Indian women and went to live among the tribes. Though the English did not do this so commonly, their relations with the Indians were at least fairly peaceful.

In Canada, as in Latin America, the government always operated under the same general attitude. The Indians were conquered peoples. In most cases, they were given reserves (like small reservations) in their original homeland. The Indian groups were small, and white settlers relatively few in number. Besides, treaties were usually made before whites moved into Indian territory, so warfare was avoided.

In the United States, it was not so simple. The earliest settlers treated Indian tribes not as captives but as separate nations, to be dealt with by treaty. When the Constitution was written it gave Congress the power "to regulate commerce . . . with the Indian tribes." The policy was to buy land from the Indians, but then leave them alone. Whites tried to work through one chief or a group of chiefs. After a satisfactory price was agreed upon, a treaty was signed. In return for giving up land, the Indians usually received yearly gifts of money or trade goods.

There were a lot of problems with this policy. Treaty-making was a new idea for Indians. They were used to making unanimous decisions. How could one person—often chosen by whites—speak for a whole tribe without every member's consent? Indians in the East and Midwest were often allowed to stay on a small portion of their former land, and got the right to hunt and fish over all the lands they sold. The whites, however, not only killed off much of the game, but they also fenced in the land for farms and kept the Indians out.

Most troublesome of all were the tribes that refused to sign the treaties. And if they really were independent nations, how could they be made to do something against their will? The answer came down to one word—force. What this meant was that Indian tribes were treated with respect as long as they did what the whites wanted them to do. When they resisted, polite ceremonies and pipe smoking gave way to rifles and cannons. And the Indians did resist. They had a long tradition of individualism and of fighting for glory.

So the United States government tried to maintain two conflicting ideas at once, treating the Indians as both independent and subservient. This confusion was mirrored in the attitudes of non-Indians. They had one myth of the Noble Savage, a dignified natural person unspoiled by civilization. And they had another myth of the Murderous Barbarian, a creature with no morals, who was little better than an animal.

There were always fair-minded people who tried to see the situation clearly. But even as intelligent a man as Thomas Jefferson could not make up his mind. At one time he wrote that "not a foot of land will ever be taken from the Indians without their consent. The sacredness of their rights is felt by all thinking persons in America." A few years later, he was predicting that the Indians would "relapse into barbarism and misery and we will be obliged to drive them with the beasts of the forest into the Rocky Mountains."

Whatever was said, there seemed to be only one aim. That was to get the Indians out of the way. Almost from the time of the landing at Jamestown, the Indians had to make way for the whites. Men like Osceola, Pontiac, and Tecumseh made a stand. The harmless Delaware moved out peacefully. But the results were the same. Those who resisted were defeated. Those who made agreements were constantly uprooted and pushed from place to place.

Indians did remain in small pockets of land in the East and Midwest. But most of those who survived kept moving west. In 1830 the federal government passed the Removal Act, which required all eastern Indians to move across the Mississippi River. They were to occupy land that was—at that time—unwanted by the whites. Americans tried to convince themselves that instead of merely pushing the Indians out of the way, the government would now try to make provision for them by granting them lands on which they could live "as long as the grass shall grow."

But the American government was only storing up trouble for itself. By the 1860s, Indians had been pushed across the Mississippi by the thousands, and they had been given enormous tracts of land. One part of this land was Indian Territory (which later became the state of Oklahoma). At first it was reserved for the "Five Civilized Tribes"—the Creek, Choctaw, Chickasaw, Seminole, and Cherokee. During the Civil War, however, these tribes sided with the Confederacy, so they were punished and much of their land was taken away and given to Woodland tribes such as the Shawnee and Potawatomi. In addition to Indian Territory, vast areas of North Dakota, South Dakota, and Montana had been set aside for the Plains tribes. Other tribes had their own land in Wyoming, Colorado, and several other western states.

The hitch was that, by the mid-1860s, Americans no longer regarded this land as undesirable. Now they wanted it, and they demanded that the Indians give up most of it with certain parts kept as reservations. The Indians were expected to move onto the reservations and stay there. This policy led to the last desperate resistance of the Navajo, Crazy Horse, Chief Joseph, and Geronimo.

By this time the United States had at last given up the idea that it was dealing with independent equals. In 1871 Congress ruled that Indian tribes were to be treated as "domestic dependent nations." Individual Indians became "wards" of the government. The "Great White Father" for the first time assumed full responsibility for their education and welfare.

The vast areas that earlier had been regarded as Indian lands were eventually reduced to some 138 million acres. This sounds like a lot, but much of the land was barren. Nevertheless, the Indians were expected to stay there no matter what. Said the Commissioner of Indian Affairs in 1872: "There is no question of national dignity involved in the treatment of savages by civilized powers. With wild men, as with wild beasts, the question of whether in a given situation one shall fight, coax, or run, is a question merely of what is easiest and safest."

Once the Indians were subdued and settled, the government wanted to make them "civilized." They were to be given animals, seeds, and tools, and taught to farm. And since their "savage" traditions would only slow down this process, they were to be "de-Indianized." They were forbidden to hold their old religious ceremonies. Tribal organizations were discouraged. Teaching in Indian languages was prohibited, and only English could be used in schools. After all, said an official, "This language which is good enough for a white man or a black man ought to be good enough for the red man." All of these rules were created to help achieve the eventual goal, assimilation. The Indians were to lose their identity as Indians and live like other Americans. A favorite saying of educators at this time was "Kill the Indian and save the man."

For some Indians, reservation life worked out fairly well. This was particularly true in the Southwest. The Pueblo had always farmed, and they continued doing so in their old locations. They put glass windows in their adobe homes, bought ready-made clothes, and adopted Christianity. (Many continued the old masked dances, though often in secret.) The Navajo took to sheep ranching with enthusiasm. The women wove fine blankets, and the men learned to make beautiful silver jewelry. The Southeast peoples, too, adjusted to their lands in Oklahoma as farmers.

For other Indians, reservation life was a calamity. The hunting and gathering tribes of the Woodlands, the Plains, and the lands farther west could not become farmers. Even if their tribes had earlier done any farming, they considered it woman's work. Hunting Indians thought plowing was degrading, and refused to "play nursemaid" to a herd of cattle. So crops withered, and the cattle died. Alcohol had been forbidden to the Indians since 1802, but they managed to get it, and to achieve drunken substitutes for the visions of old. Many simply clustered around the agency, the headquarters of the federally appointed agent who administered the reservation. They lived on the beef rations the agent handed out periodically.

In the midst of their despair, these Indians heard a voice of hope. It came from yet another "prophet," in the tradition of Tecumseh's brother and of the man who had inspired Pontiac. Around 1870, a Nevada Paiute named Wovoka began preaching that the old life would be restored. Whites would disappear, he predicted. Game would be plentiful again. He taught his followers a ritual, the Ghost Dance, during which the dancers, in a sort of trance, felt themselves to be reunited with their dead relatives and friends. Wovoka won a few followers among the Basin-Plateau and California peoples, but not many.

In the 1880s, however, the Plains Indians heard of Wovoka's teachings and added something new. Wovoka had preached peace, which was not acceptable to the warlike people of the Plains. The whites would not disappear, they said, unless the Indians killed them. The Sioux developed a

The Ghost Dance shirt was covered with designs that were supposed to ward off bullets. This Pawnee garment of buckskin was painted blue on top and red on the bottom, with white stars.

special Ghost Dance shirt that was supposed to repel bullets by magic. From this point on, the Ghost Dance movement spread like wildfire.

Throughout 1889 and 1890, the Indians danced. The whites were afraid that the dancing was done in preparation for war. They brought 3,000 troops into South Dakota. In one skirmish, Indian "police" forces employed by the whites killed Sitting Bull, who had returned from Canada a few years earlier. Now there was panic on both sides. Late in 1890 a group of Sioux decided to travel to the agency on the Pine Ridge reservation. On their way, they stopped and pitched camp at a creek known as Wounded Knee.

On December 29, government soldiers surrounded the Sioux tipis and demanded surrender. In the midst of negotiations, a gun was fired, and the "battle" of Wounded Knee had begun. It was the dying gasp of Indian resistance in the United States. The Indians were outnumbered and doomed, but they killed 25 soldiers. Of the Sioux at least 146 were killed, many of them women and children. A Sioux who went to Wounded Knee to bury the dead recalled, years later:

> After the soldiers marched away from their dirty work, a heavy snow began to fall. The wind came up in the night. There was a big blizzard, and it grew very cold. The snow drifted deep in the crooked gulch, and it was one long grave of butchered women and children and babies, who had never done any harm and were only trying to run away.[1]

That was the end of the Ghost Dance. Afterward came greater apathy and despair than ever before.

Meanwhile the federal government had decided on another plan to encourage assimilation. The Dawes Act of 1887 aimed at breaking up reservations entirely. Every adult Indian was given 160 acres, every child under the age of 18 was given 80 acres. Whatever land was left over after allotment was sold to whites. The Indians themselves were

allowed to sell their land after twenty-five years if they were
judged competent to manage their own affairs.

The result was disastrous. Eager whites swooped down
on the land like locusts. They bought up thousands of acres.
Why did the Indians sell, if land meant so much to them that
they had fought to the death over it? One answer is that the
land they sold was not always the land they had fought for.
It might be a dry plot hundreds of miles from their original
home.

Another answer was given in an official government
report: "The Indian by tradition was not concerned with
possession, did not worry about titles or recordings, but
regarded the land as a fisherman might regard the sea, as a
gift of nature, to be loved and feared, to be fought and
revered, and to be drawn on by all as an inexhaustible source
of life and strength."

Then, too, good crisp dollar bills looked much better to
many Indians than a few square miles of dusty plain. That
the dollars would soon give out did not concern them, for
they were not in the habit of long-range planning. While the
Dawes Act was in effect (about forty years), the 138 million
acres of Indian land dwindled to 52 million. Thousands of
Indians sank into the deepest poverty.

By the 1920s, it was obvious to many people that
something had to be done. Pushing the Indians out of the
way had not worked. Neither had putting them on reservations, nor casting them into the white world without any
preparation. One sign of change was that Indians were
granted citizenship in 1924, though they were not allowed to
vote until 1940. More important was the Wheeler-Howard
(or Indian Reorganization) Act of 1934, called the "Indian
New Deal." Its aim was to encourage Indians to organize
themselves and run their own affairs. Tribes could incorpo-
rate and own land in common. The sale of land to non-
Indians was forbidden. Indian languages could be taught,
and old crafts and traditions were fostered. Indian tribes
were regarded as the ruling authorities on their own lands.

In the period that followed, Indians regained some of
their pride and self-respect. They wrote tribal constitutions,
elected officers, and proved that they did not have to

depend on the whites for everything. They developed tribal businesses that helped their standard of living. For example, the Apache on the San Carlos reservation in Arizona did well as cattle ranchers. The discovery of oil, uranium, and gas on several reservations brought in needed funds, though too often the money was simply parceled out to individual families and spent in a few years.

One basic difficulty remained. While the Indian population was increasing, Indian land was fixed in size. Much reservation territory was not very good to begin with, and it could not support growing numbers of people. In Canada, where tribes like the Cree and Chipewyan had become dependent on the fur trade, their livelihood disappeared when the demand for furs dwindled. Thousands became dependent on government rations instead.

In the early 1950s the American government announced yet another solution for the "Indian problem." This was a policy of termination and relocation. Reservations were to be ended as such, with the land becoming part of the state in which it was located. And Indians were to be relocated to ease population pressure and to foster assimilation. After preliminary training in various skills, many Indians were resettled in urban areas such as Los Angeles and Chicago.

Termination and relocation didn't work out very well, either. Indians resisted attempts to close down their reservations. Those who did relocate in urban centers were not happy there. Big cities can be cold and impersonal places. Indians—many of them uneducated and unskilled—had trouble finding jobs. Many of them turned to their old consolation, alcohol (legal since 1953). According to some estimates, as many as 90 percent of "relocatees" returned to their reservations. One example shows the extent of the problem. The Mohawk turned out to be excellent structural steel workers on bridges and skyscrapers because they seemed to have no fear of heights. But even they continued to return to their reserve in Canada every summer. If they died far from "home," their bodies were returned to the reserve for burial.

In 1970 President Nixon announced yet another

federal policy for Indians, "self-determination without termination." One sign of this shift was that some 40 million acres of Alaskan land was turned over to the Indians. And Indians themselves were becoming more militant. Like many other minorities, they were taking a new pride in their identity. They saw their own heritage as an asset, not something to be ashamed of—"red power," some called it. Indians staged protests that received wide publicity. They occupied Alcatraz Island in 1969, and vandalized the Bureau of Indian Affairs in Washington in 1972. The following year they seized the town of Wounded Knee, South Dakota, and issued demands for radical changes. In 1978 they staged a cross-country trek, the "Longest Walk," to Washington, D.C., to dramatize their problems.

Probably more important than these "media events" was a new organization, the Native American Rights Fund. It launched a series of lawsuits that showed that native Americans were far from being a "vanishing race." Tribes that had been forgotten for decades seemed to spring out of the soil with new vigor: the Penobscot and Passamaquoddy of Maine, the Wampanoag of Massachusetts, the Abnaki of Vermont, the Catawba of South Carolina, the Nisqually of Washington. They went to court to fight for land, water, and fishing rights that had seemingly been lost forever. And, often, they won.

And more "visible" Indians, like the Navajo, showed a new militancy in regard to such issues as mineral rights. Indian lands in the West contain not only oil and uranium, but also huge amounts of coal. With the energy crisis of the 1970s, some Indian leaders backed a movement to demand far higher payments for the resources exploited by American mining companies. By the late 1970s it was clear that, whatever their problems, American Indians were a special people who would not be swallowed up without leaving a trace.

Of the million Indians in the United States today, about 650,000 live on or near federal reservations. These are located in twenty-five states, most of them west of the

Mississippi River. The rest live among the general population, except for a few who live on state reservations in the East.

Much reservation land is desert or semidesert. In the late 1960s the Bureau of Indian Affairs issued a report on the 56 million acres of federal reservation land that then belonged to the Indians. Of this total, it said, 14 million acres were "critically eroded" and 17 million acres were "severely eroded." The remaining 25 million acres were "slightly eroded." Since farming or ranching on such land is difficult at best, other means of livelihood have been tried. Industries have set up factories on or near reservations, and mining and extracting operations also provide work for Indians. But there are not nearly enough jobs for everyone.

The very policy of maintaining reservations has a built-in problem. Two ideas are at odds with one another. On the one hand, Indian tribes are supposed to be completely independent in running their own affairs. On the other hand, they benefit from government protection that is not available to other Americans. For example, their land is not taxed. It cannot be sold, rented, or given away without the consent both of the Indians and the federal government. This protection obviously involves a certain amount of supervision. How can people be truly free when they still have to rely on special help for their survival?

On or off reservations, there is still something left of the old Indian attitudes about life, the search for oneness with nature. Some Indians have accepted Christianity and kept their traditional ways, too. Others have developed a new sort of religion that combines Christianity with the vision quest. They call it the Native American Church. It is built around peyote, a cactus plant also known as mescal. The peyote has a small "button" top that is cut off and dried. When chewed or steeped in tea, it produces visions.

The Indians in Mexico have been using peyote for centuries, but the custom spread into the United States only in the late 1800s. The Plains tribes took it up enthusiastically, as they did the Ghost Dance. It then spread to many other tribes as well. The cult built around peyote involves all-night sessions with many rituals. Sometimes peyote is not even chewed, but simply placed on an altar. Often there is Bible reading. In the morning there is a big feast.

There are still Indians who reject Christianity in any form, and cling fiercely to their old beliefs. As a Hopi put it: "Other gods may help some people, but my only chance for a good life is with the gods of my fathers. I will never forsake them, even though their ceremonies die out before my eyes and all their shrines are neglected."

Sooner or later, no matter where they live, how (or whether) they work and worship, Indians come face to face with their most difficult problem. This is the conflict of values that has come with the clash of Indian and "white" cultures. Many white Americans have long expected that their own ways would win out, and that Indians would somehow stop being Indians. There has been strong pressure to conform, and to blend into the American "melting pot." But many Indians (like many other Americans) dislike the urban mass society they are being asked to fit into.

For these Indians, it is extremely important to be among their own people and aware of their tribal identity. They are able to surround themselves with friends and relatives with whom they can share a feeling of hospitality, generosity, and the unhurried enjoyment of the moment. An Indian boy away at college says, "My tribe is within me. It gives me strength." It is this sense of community that most Indians want and need. No matter how poor or rejected, they want to feel pride in being Indian. A girl from a New Mexico pueblo spoke of the future:

> If I were living in a dream world what would I want? I would want my people to be able to hold on to our beautiful way of life. I would want my people to hold on to their ways somehow, and yet be able to be on the same level as the white man. I would want my people to live in our way. If I were living in a dream world that is what I would want.[2]

Perhaps in the real world her dream can come true. An Oregon Indian is optimistic:

> We will survive. We were here for twenty thousand years, at least. We were given this land by the Great Spirit. If we can endure all that we've endured, and still be here, we'll be here in the future.[3]

NOTES

CHAPTER 1

1.   Margot Astrov, *American Indian Prose and Poetry* (New York: Putnam's, Capricorn, 1962), pp. 245-46, quoting Leo Simmons, *Sun Chief, The Autobiography of a Hopi Indian.*

CHAPTER 2

1.   Thomas Jefferson, *Notes on the State of Virginia* (Philadelphia: Prichard and Hall, 1788), pp. 103–06. Adapted.
2.   Ibid.
3.   Ibid.
4.   Roger C. Owen et al., *The North American Indians* (New York: Macmillan, 1967), p. 546, quoting Penicault.
5.   Ibid., p. 548, quoting Le Petit.

CHAPTER 4

1.   Jack D. Forbes, ed., *The Indian in America's Past* (Englewood Cliffs, N.J.: Prentice-Hall, 1964), pp. 59-60, quoting from *Lives of Celebrated American Indians*, 1843.

CHAPTER 5

1.   Samuel Hearne, *A Journey from Prince of Wales's Fort in Hudson's Bay to the Northern Ocean* (New York: Macmillan, 1958), p. xix.
2.   Richard Slobodin, "Kutchin Concepts of Reincarnation," *Western Canadian Journal of Anthropology*, vol. II, no. 1 (1971), p. 67.

CHAPTER 6

1. Thomas Mails, *The Mystic Warriors of the Plains* (Garden City, N.Y.: Doubleday, 1973), quoting Maximilian of Wied, p. 27. Slightly adapted.
2. Forbes, op cit., p. 65, quoting Neihardt, *Black Elk Speaks*.
3. Mark Brown and W. R. Felton, *The Frontier Years* (New York: Clarkson N. Potter, Bramhall House, 1955), p. 65, quoting Granville Stuart.

CHAPTER 7

1. All quotes from Lewis and Clark's journals in this chapter, taken from Meriwether Lewis and William Clark, *Journals* (New York: Antiquarian Press, 1959), passim.
2. Astrov, p. 85.
3. Ibid., p. 87.

CHAPTER 9

1. R. F. Heizer and M. A. Whipple, *The California Indians* (Berkeley, Calif.: University of California Press, 1951), pp. 482–83, quoting Waterman.
2. Theodora Kroeber, *Ishi in Two Worlds* (Berkeley, Calif.: University of California Press, 1965), pp. 237–38.
3. Harold E. Driver, *Indians of North America* (Chicago: University of Chicago Press, 1961), quoting Stephen Powers, *Tribes of California*, 1877.

CHAPTER 10

1. Forbes, op. cit., p. 50, quoting Neihardt, *Black Elk Speaks*.
2. Stan Steiner, *The New Indians* (New York: Harper & Row, 1968), p. 289.
3. Earl Shorris, *The Death of the Great Spirit* (New York: Simon & Schuster, 1971), p. 144.

BIBLIOGRAPHY

For Further Reading

Astrov, Margot, ed. *American Indian Prose and Poetry.* New York: Putnam's, Capricorn, 1962. A large selection from both North and South America.

Bierhorst, John, ed. *The Red Swan: Myths and Tales of the American Indian.* New York: Farrar, Straus, 1976. Includes stories from many different tribes.

Brown, Dee. *Bury My Heart at Wounded Knee.* New York: Holt, Rinehart & Winston, 1971. An Indian view of Western settlement.

David, Jay, ed. *The American Indian: The First Victim.* New York: Morrow, 1972. Indians' own accounts of growing up Indian.

Deloria, Vine. *Custer Died for Your Sins: An Indian Manifesto.* New York: Macmillan, 1969. Indictment of American policies by a Sioux spokesman.

Deuel, Leo. *Conquistadors Without Swords: Archaeologists in the Americas.* New York: St. Martin's, 1967. Essays on outstanding discoveries, from Spanish times to the present.

Dockstader, Frederick J. *Great North American Indians.* New York: Van Nostrand, 1977. Illustrated biographies of scores of well-known Indians.

————. *Indian Art in America: The Arts and Crafts of the North American Indian.* New York: Promontory Press, 1973. Many color pictures.

Drucker, Philip. *Indians of the Northwest Coast.* American Museum Science Books. Garden City, N.Y.: Doubleday, Natural History Press, 1963. A comprehensive survey.

Feder, Norman. *American Indian Art.* New York: Abrams, 1971. Lavishly illustrated.

Forbes, Jack D., ed. *The Indian in America's Past.* Englewood Cliffs, N.J.: Prentice-Hall, 1964. Large selection of short documents.

Hamilton, Charles. *Cry of the Thunderbird: The American Indian's Own Story.* Norman, Okla.: University of Oklahoma Press, 1972. Includes sketches by several Indian artists.

Josephy, Alvin M., Jr., ed. *American Heritage Book of Indians.* New York: American Heritage, 1961. A popular survey by major culture areas.

Kickingbird, Kirke, and Duchéneaux, Karen. *One Hundred Million Acres.* New York: Macmillan, 1973. A critique of Indian land policy.

Kubiak, William J. *Great Lakes Indians: A Pictorial Guide.* Grand Rapids, Mich.: Baker Book House, 1970. Tribe-by-tribe summary, with many drawings.

Lowie, Robert H. *Indians of the Plains.* American Museum Science Books. Garden City, N.Y.: Doubleday, Natural History Press, 1963. A comprehensive survey.

Mails, Thomas. *The Mystic Warriors of the Plains.* Garden City, N.Y.: Doubleday, 1973. Handsome volume with many drawings.

Macgowan, Kenneth, and Hester, Joseph A., Jr. *Early Man in the New World.* Natural History Library Edition. Garden City, N.Y.: Doubleday, 1962. Detailed but clear analysis of Indian origins.

McLuhan, T. C., ed. *Touch the Earth: A Self-Portrait of Indian Existence.* New York: Outerbridge & Dienstfrey, 1971. Poetic extracts, with photos by Edward Curtis.

Marriott, Alice, and Rachlin, Carol. *American Indian Mythol-*

ogy. New York: Crowell, 1968. Retelling of many legends and stories.

Moquin, Wayne, ed. *Great Documents in American Indian History.* New York: Praeger, 1973. In three parts: "The Indian Way," "Captive Nations," and "Heading Toward the Mainstream."

Muench, David, and Pike, Donald G. *Anasazi: Ancient People of the Rock.* Palo Alto, Calif.: American West, 1974. Many beautiful color photographs.

National Geographic on Indians of the Americas. Washington, D.C.: National Geographic Society, 1955. Re-creations of Indian life through 149 paintings.

Neithammer, Carolyn. *Daughters of the Earth: The Lives and Legends of American Indian Women.* New York: Macmillan, 1977. Wide-ranging text embellished with folktales and poetry.

Ritzenthaler, Robert E., and Ritzenthaler, Pat. *The Woodland Indians.* American Museum Science Books. Garden City, N.Y.: Doubleday, Natural History Press, 1970. A comprehensive survey.

Shorris, Earl. *The Death of the Great Spirit: An Elegy for the American Indian.* New York: Simon & Schuster, 1971. Sensitive portrayal of Indians in the modern world.

Symington, Fraser. *The Canadian Indian: The Illustrated History of the Great Tribes of Canada.* Toronto: McClelland & Stewart, 1969. A heavily illustrated survey.

Tillett, Leslie, ed. *Wind on the Buffalo Grass: The Indians' Own Account of the Battle at the Little Big Horn River, and the Death of Their Life on the Plains.* New York: Crowell, 1976. Illustrated with drawings by Indians who took part.

Tunis, Edwin. *Indians.* Cleveland: World, 1959. Drawings focus on Indian art and technology.

Vanderwerth, W. C., ed. *Indian Oratory: Famous Speeches by Noted Indian Chieftains.* Norman, Okla.: University of Oklahoma Press, 1971. Each of the 35 speeches is preceded by a short biography.

Vogel, Virgil J. *This Country Was Ours.* New York: Harper & Row, 1972. A documentary history of American Indians.

Washburn, Wilcomb E. *The Indian in America*. New York: Harper & Row, 1975. Emphasizes historic times.

Wied-Neuwied, Prince Maximilian of. *People of the First Man*. New York: Dutton, 1976. Present-day editors have combined travel accounts by a German prince with a portfolio of watercolors by Karl Bodmer.

INDEX